Robot Computational Dispersion and Exploration on Graph Topologies And Performance Indices

By

Robin Kenth

Contents

Chapter 1

Introduction

A considerable amount of research has been devoted in recent years to the study of distributed algorithms for autonomous multi-robot system. A multi-robot system, which are collectively referred to as *robot swarms* consists of a set of autonomous mobile computational entities, called *robots*, that coordinate with each other to achieve some well defined goals, such as forming a given pattern, exploration of unknown environments etc. These robot swarms draw inspiration from the coordinated behaviors observed in nature such as ant colonies, swarms of bees, the collective movements of fish, the flocking of birds, and more [11, 76, 101, 103]. Despite the individual entities in these biological swarms having limited capabilities, they can collectively achieve complex objectives through group interactions.

The primary goal of swarm robotics is to replicate this concept by creating a system consisting of a large number of uncomplicated, generic robots. These robots work together to perform complex tasks without relying on centralized control mechanisms. Since there's no central control, robot swarms operate as distributed systems, meaning that each robot independently executes an algorithm based on its own observations.

The utilization of swarms composed of low-cost, less powerful, and uncomplicated robots is emerging as a practical substitute for employing a solitary, high-powered, and expensive robot. This strategy offers numerous benefits compared to traditional single-robot approaches. The production of a single advanced robot with intricate structure and control systems can be prohibitively costly. In contrast, the individual components of a robot swarm, characterized by their simplicity and generality, are economical and can be manufactured in large quantities. Consequently, even if a swarm comprises a substantial number of such robots, it can still be notably more budget-friendly than a solitary powerful robot.

In specific tasks where recovering and reusing robots after completion isn't feasible, opting for expensive robots becomes economically unfeasible. In such scenarios, robot swarms present a suitable alternative solution. Additionally, swarming offers advantages in terms of stability and resilience compared to single-robot systems. A malfunction in a single robot's component can significantly impede its functionality, whereas a swarm can continue progressing toward its objective even if some individual robots encounter issues or cease working. This ability to withstand malfunctions or faults makes robot swarms especially appealing for addressing large-scale tasks in hostile or hazardous environments.

Due to its potential applications across a wide array of practical challenges, such that robotics [8,10,47,102], control [19,46,69,70], Artificial Intelligence [53,54,68], engineering [59,104] and other large scale problems [1,60,75,82,96,97,107], the distributed coordination of robot swarms has garnered substantial research attention. Early explorations in this field were primarily undertaken within the artificial intelligence community where, one of the initial studies within this community demonstrated how basic local interactions among swarm members could result in intricate global behaviors. Additional investigations within the AI domain examined scenarios where simple autonomous robots were tasked with collecting and aggregating objects distributed within a rectangular region. These studies aimed to showcase the effectiveness of stigmergic communication among the robots. There were also alternative approaches explored within the AI community, such as planner-based architectures, information requirement theory, and Swarm Intelligence. These approaches shared the common trait of being experimental in nature, with a focus on demonstrating practical outcomes rather than formal correctness proofs for the algorithms.

In contrast, within the distributed computing community, the study of robot swarms was primarily approached the subject from a computational standpoint, seeking to understand how different robot features and capabilities related to the solvability of tasks. Subsequently, there has been a series of theoretical inquiries into the computational aspects of robot swarms from a distributed computing perspective. In these theoretical studies, the primary goal is to determine the minimum capabilities required for robots to solve specific problems. The emphasis in these works lies in rigorous mathematical proofs rather than empirical or experimental evidence. The overarching aim of this research is to gain a clear understanding of how various robot attributes and capabilities, such as memory, communication, sensing, synchronization, and agreement among local coordinate systems, interact with the swarm's computability. For example, we have dedicated one of the chapters in understanding the difference in computational capabilities of a robot swarm acting under *full visibility* and *limited visibility* conditions.

Traditionally the spatial environments in which autonomous mobile entities operate can be classified into two fundamental settings. The first setting, which is the discrete setting is where the domain is represented by a simple graph. This setting is suitable for scenarios like mobile robots in communication networks [24, 58].

The second setting or the continuous setting is where the domain is a connected region of $\mathbb{R}^2$ or Euclidean plane. This setting is applicable to situations where robots traverse a continuous terrain or navigate through space. In the context of the continuous universe, extensive research efforts have been conducted within distinct communities of researchers [7, 8, 10, 19, 47, 68]. These efforts have given rise to the well-established and mature field of autonomous mobile robots, which encompasses areas such as swarm robotics, robotic networks, and mobile sensor networks. Researchers from various disciplines, including robotics, control systems, artificial intelligence, engineering, and more recently, distributed computing, have contributed to advancing this field.

In Section 1.1, we give an overview of standard models of robot swarms considered in theoretical studies. In Section 1.2, we discuss the earlier works in this direction. Section 1.3 gives a brief overview of the thesis.

1.1 Theoretical Framework

This section provides an overview of the theoretical framework under which the computational and complexity issues related to distributed computing by robot swarms are studied. The framework covers a large spectrum of settings. The different sets of assumptions regarding the capabilities of the robots and the environment in which they operate give rise to several variations of the framework.

1.1.1 The Robots

We consider a team $R = \{r_0, \ldots, r_n\}$ of computational entities which are viewed as points and called *robots*. The robots can move freely and continuously. The robots can operate in discrete domain represented by a simple graph or in continuous domain represented by Euclidean Plane $\mathbb{R}^2$. The graph may be *static*, where there is no change in the nodes and links of the graph, or it may be *dynamic*, where there may be change in the links or edges.

First of all we define some common terms which will be frequently used in our discussion:

1. *anonymous*: The robots do not have unique identifiers.
2. *identical*: The robots are indistinguishable by their appearance.
3. *homogenous*: All the robots execute the same algorithm.
4. *autonomous*: The robots act without any centralized control.

We have considered three different problems in this thesis and hence the overall characteristics of the robot swarms have varied according to the problems.

A robot may or not have distinct identifiers, which are usually bit strings of constant length distinguishing one robot from the other. When the robots do not have distinct identifiers they are called *anonymous* as mentioned above. When the underlying domain is the Euclidean Plane, robots can move freely and continuously in the plane. If the underlying domain is a static graph then a robot can move from one node to a neighbouring node freely. When the underlying domain is a dynamic graph, robot can move from one node to a neighbouring node if the edge between them is not missing. Two robots moving in opposite direction on the same edge are not able to detect each other.

The robots may or may not have any persistent memory. When the robots do not have any memory they are called *oblivious*. They do not remember any data from the previous round. When the robots do have persistent memory they can only save finite bits of information from the previous round.

The communication between the robots can be of various types. There may be no communication at all, while on the other hand there may be *local* communication or even more powerful *global* communication. In the graph models we have considered in this thesis, irrespective of static or dynamic, the communication is *local*, the communication between two robots is possible if and only if they are co-located at a node. In Chapter 5, where we have considered Euclidean Plane, communication if at all present is in the form of *lights*.

Each robot has its own local coordinate system and it always perceives itself at its origin; there might not be consistency between these coordinate systems.

1.1.2 Look-Compute-Move Cycle

The robots do not have access to any global coordinate system. Each robot has its own local coordinate system, whose origin always coincides with the position of the robot and hence it changes with the robot as it moves. The robots operate in $Look - Compute - Move$ (LCM) cycles. When activated a robot executes a cycle by performing the following three operations:

1. *Look*: The robots activate its sensors to obtain a snapshot of the positions occupied by the robots according to its co-ordinate system.

2. *Compute*: The robot executes its algorithm using the snapshot as input. The result of the computation is a destination point.

3. *Move*: The robot moves to the computed destination. If the destination is the current location, the robot stays still.

All robots are initially idle. The amount of time to complete a cycle is assumed to be finite, and the *Look* is assumed to be instantaneous. The robots may not have any agreement in terms of their local coordinate system.

1.1.3 Visibility

Each robot is capable of observing its surroundings. There are three main models regarding the visibility of the robots.

Full visibility: In *full visibility* model, the robots have sensorial devices that allows it to observe the positions of the other robots in its local co-ordinate system.

Limited visibility: In *limited visibility* model, a robot can only observe upto a fixed distance V_r from it. Suppose, $r_p(t)$ denote the position of a robot r at the beginning of round t. Then we define the circle with center at $r_p(t)$ and radius V_r to be the *Circle of Visibility* of r at round t. Here the radius V_r is same for all the robots. The result of *Look* operation in round t will be the position of the robots and lights(if any) of the robots inside the circle of visibility.

We now define the *Visibility Graph*, $G = (V, E)$ of a configuration. Let C be a given configuration. Then all the robot positions become the vertices of G and we say an edge exists between any two vertices if and only if the robots present there can see each other. A necessary condition for a robot swarm trying to solve a problem collectively is that the *Visibility Graph* of the initial configuration must be connected.

Obstructed visibility: In the *obstructed visibility* or *opaque robot* model, the visibility range of each robot is unlimited, but its visibility can be obstructed by the presence of other robots. Formally, two robots are able to see each other if and only if no other robot lies on the line segment joining them.

1.1.4 Memory and Communication

Based on the memory and communication capabilities, there are four models: $\mathcal{OBLOT}, \mathcal{LUMI}, \mathcal{FSTA}$ and $\mathcal{FCOM}$.

$\mathcal{OBLOT}$: One of the most widely explored and well-established models in this context is referred to as $\mathcal{OBLOT}$. In this model, robots are characterized as both silent and oblivious. When we say robots are *silent*, it means that they lack explicit communication capabilities. Additionally, when we describe them as *oblivious*, it implies that they possess no memory of prior observations, calculations, or actions. In other words, at the conclusion of each cycle involving looking, computing, and moving, all information acquired during that cycle, including observations, computations, and actions taken, is completely erased. Consequently, any computations made during a cycle are solely based on what is observed in the current cycle, without any retention of past data or actions.

$\mathcal{LUMI}$: In this model, each robot is equipped with a visible light that can take on a finite number of predefined colors. This light is not only visible to the robot itself but also to other nearby robots. These lights serve a dual purpose as a limited form of explicit communication and a kind of memory for the robots. During the LOOK phase, a robot observes the positions of other robots that are within its visibility range, along with the colors of their lights, as well as the color of its own light. Subsequently, based on this information, the robot performs computations using a designated algorithm to determine both a destination point and a color. The robot then changes the color of its light to the chosen one and moves to the computed destination.

One crucial feature is that the color of a robot's light persists from one $LOOK - COMPUTE - MOVE$ cycle to the next. This means that the chosen color is not erased at the end of a cycle and is retained when the robot enters the LOOK phase of the subsequent cycle. It's worth noting that a robot equipped with a light that has only one possible color effectively behaves the same as a robot with no light at all. Consequently, the $\mathcal{LUMI}$ model represents an extension of the $\mathcal{OBLOT}$ model, offering more capabilities due to the introduction of persistent, multicolored lights.

$\mathcal{FSTA}$: In the $\mathcal{FSTA}$ model, robots share a common characteristic with $\mathcal{OBLOT}$ in that they are silent, but they differ by having finite memory. Each robot in $\mathcal{FSTA}$ is equipped with a light, but unlike $\mathcal{LUMI}$, this light is only visible to the robot itself. During the LOOK phase, a robot observes the positions of other robots within its field of view but cannot perceive the colors of their lights. However, it can see the color of its own light. Following this observation, the robot engages in computations using a specified algorithm to determine both a destination point and a color. Subsequently, the robot adjusts its light to match the chosen color and moves to the calculated destination.

It's important to note that in $\mathcal{FSTA}$, robots can only perceive the color of their own light and not the lights of other robots, setting it apart from $\mathcal{LUMI}$. Nevertheless, if a robot in $\mathcal{FSTA}$ has a light with only one available color, its capabilities become equivalent to those of a robot in the $\mathcal{OBLOT}$ model.

$\mathcal{FCOM}$: In the $\mathcal{FCOM}$ model, robots share a common characteristic with $\mathcal{OBLOT}$ in that they are oblivious, but they have a finite number of communication bits at their disposal. Similar to $\mathcal{LUMI}$, each robot in $\mathcal{FCOM}$ is equipped with a light. However, there is a distinction in that a robot's light is only visible to other robots and not to itself. During the LOOK phase, a robot observes the positions of other robots within its field of view, including the colors of their lights, but it cannot perceive the color of its own light. Subsequently, based on this observation, the robot executes computations using a designated algorithm to determine both a destination point and a color. The robot then adjusts its light to match the chosen color and moves to the calculated destination.

It's important to highlight that in $\mathcal{FCOM}$, robots can see the lights of other robots but not the color of their own light, setting it apart from $\mathcal{LUMI}$.

However, if a robot in $\mathcal{FCOM}$ has a light with only one available color, its capabilities are essentially the same as those of a robot in the $\mathcal{OBLOT}$ model.

1.1.5 Activation and Synchronization

Based on the activation and timing of action of the robots, there are three models: fully synchronous ($\mathcal{FSYNC}$), semi-synchronous ($\mathcal{SSYNC}$) and asynchronous ($\mathcal{ASYNC}$).

Fully synchronous: In model, time is conceptually divided into discrete global rounds. During each of these rounds, all the robots are simultaneously activated. They collectively take snapshots of their surroundings at the same moment, and subsequently, they carry out their movements in a synchronized manner. Consequently, the $LOOK$, $COMPUTE$, and $MOVE$ phases of the robots are coordinated and occur concurrently within these global rounds.

Semi-synchronous: The $\mathcal{SSYNC}$ model aligns with the model $\mathcal{FSYNC}$, differing only in the aspect that not all robots are necessarily activated during every round. However, it's important to note that in the $\mathcal{SSYNC}$ model, each robot is guaranteed to be activated infinitely many times over time.

Asynchronous: The $\mathcal{ASYNC}$ model represents the most general and flexible framework. In this model, robots are activated independently, and each robot carries out its cycles without synchronization with others. The duration of time spent in $LOOK$, $COMPUTE$, $MOVE$, and inactive states is finite but not limited or predictable. Importantly, this duration can vary between different robots and is not uniform. Consequently, the robots lack a common, synchronized notion of time.

In this $\mathcal{ASYNC}$ model, certain unique characteristics emerge. For instance, a robot can be observed while in motion, which means computations may be based on outdated information regarding positions. Additionally, the configuration perceived by a robot during the LOOK phase can undergo significant changes before the robot actually executes its move. This level of unpredictability and asynchrony makes the $\mathcal{ASYNC}$ model the most versatile but also the most challenging among the considered models.

1.1.6 Movement of the Robots

The movement of the robots in each of the three domains: Euclidean plane, static graph and dynamic graph are different.

In our study in Euclidean plane domain usually the robots are assumed to move along straight line. In $\mathcal{FSYNC}$ and $\mathcal{SSYNC}$, the speed of the robot is not important as all movements terminate before the next global round starts. However, certain studies also allow the robots to move along curved trajectories. However, in $\mathcal{ASYNC}$, the speed determines the duration of the MOVE operation of the robot in that LOOK-COMPUTE-MOVE cycle. Regardless of the speed, the movement of a robot may stop before the robot reaches its destination. In this regard, there are two main models.

Rigid: In the RIGID movement model, each robot can travel to its intended destination without any interruptions or disruptions.

Non-Rigid: In the NON-RIGID movement model, In the Non-Rigid movement model, a robot's movement may come to a halt before it reaches its intended destination. However, within this model, there exists a specific distance parameter, denoted as $\delta > 0$ (where $\delta > 0$), that plays a crucial role. Here are the key properties related to δ:

If the robot's destination is at a distance no greater than δ, then the robot is guaranteed to reach that destination without interruption.

If the robot's destination is at a distance greater than $\delta > 0$, the robot will travel at least the distance $\delta > 0$ toward the destination before any potential halt or interruption occurs.

The inclusion of this distance parameter, $\delta > 0$, is essential because it ensures that the model does not permit frequent interruptions after covering distances like $\frac{1}{2}, \frac{1}{4}, \frac{1}{8}, \ldots$, and so on. Without δ, the model would not allow any robot to traverse a distance greater than 1. Importantly, whether the value of δ is known to the robots or not may vary within this model.

If the underlying domain is a static graph then a robot can move from one node to an adjacent node. Any number of robots are allowed to move via an edge. If the graph is port-labelled, i.e, it's edges have port numbers then when a robot moves from a node u to node v, it is aware of the port through which it enters v.

When the underlying domain is a dynamic graph, robot can move from one node to a neighbouring node if the edge between them is not missing. Two robots moving in opposite direction on the same edge are not able to detect each other.

1.2 Related Literature

In this section, a comprehensive overview of theoretical studies related to distributed computing by robot swarms is presented. The primary focus in this field is to accomplish tasks in a distributed manner. Over the past two decades, significant attention has been dedicated to the study of various problems such as PATTERN FORMATION [14, 21, 99, 105] , POINT FORMATION [4, 13, 22, 23, 33, 38, 42, 82, 86], LINE FORMATION [88, 95, 106] , CIRCLE FORMATION [12, 28, 29, 31, 35, 37, 40, 98] , CONVEX HULL FORMATION [52, 90, 92, 93], MUTUAL VISIBILITY [2, 6, 32, 72, 85].

The Pattern Formation problem entails robots being provided with a desired pattern represented as coordinate points within a coordinate system. The robots, however, lack knowledge of the global coordinate system associated with these points. To address this problem, the first step involves developing a strategy that enables all robots to agree on a global coordinate system. Subsequently, the robots must be placed sequentially at their respective destinations. The prescribed pattern can take various forms, such as a point, a line, a circle, or any arbitrary shape. In general, for a fixed pattern, the robots are not provided with specific coordinate points.

The Point Formation problem, also known as GATHERING, requires robots to converge at an unknown point. Similarly, there are Line Formation, Circle Formation, and Convex Hull Formation problems. In the Convex Hull Formation problem, robots are arranged in a way that ensures mutual visibility among all robots, a concept referred to as Mutual Visibility. It's important to note that solving the Mutual Visibility problem doesn't automatically solve the Convex Hull Formation problem. However, achieving Convex Hull Formation results in a mutually visible pattern. Solving these problems heavily relies on the spatial universe, the scheduling of robot actions, and the robots' working memory.

Fundamental problems like Gathering, Arbitrary Pattern Formation, and Mutual Visibility have been extensively studied in grid environments. In contrast, the Line Formation and Circle Formation problems have mainly been investigated in continuous Euclidean planes. The Line Formation problem serves as a foundation for solving more complex problems like Convex Hull Formation and Pattern Formation. In [15], an intermediate configuration is introduced where all robots except one form a line segment. The Line Formation problem was first discussed in [106] using a different model. In [88], the problem is examined concerning total agreement and partial agreement on the coordinate system. The Line Formation problem is also connected to spreading problem, where robots initially placed arbitrarily on the plane need to spread evenly within a given region. This study focuses on the one-dimensional case, where robots must form a line and position themselves uniformly on it.

The Circle Formation problem requires robots to position themselves along a circular circumference. If robots are evenly spaced on the circumference, it's known as UNIFORM CIRCLE FORMATION. Early work on Circle Formation was presented by Sugihara and Suzuki [98], who proposed a heuristic distributed algorithm. Later improvements were made by Tanaka [100], Suzuki and Yamasihita [99], and Défago and Konogaya [28], considering various scenarios involving robot memory and coordination. These studies often assumed synchronization models and made specific assumptions about the robots' abilities.

The Mutual Visibility problem, which involves ensuring that all robots are visible to each other, was first addressed by Di Luna et al. [32] in continuous Euclidean planes. They achieved Mutual Visibility by forming a convex N-gon, where N is the number of robots. Later work by Sharma et al. [91] improved the algorithm's round complexity in the Fsync model. The problem was also explored with luminous robots in [72], introducing more complexities regarding robot memory and synchronization.

DISPERSION was introduced in [9] where the problem was considered in specific graph structures such as paths, rings, trees as well as arbitrary graphs. In [9], the authors assumed $k = n$, i.e., the number of robots k is equal to the number of nodes n. They proved a memory lower bound of $\Omega(\log k)$ bits at each robot and a time lower bound of $\Omega(\log D)$ rounds for any deterministic algorithm to solve the problem in a graph of diameter D. They then provided deterministic algorithms using $O(\log n)$ bits of memory at each robot to solve DISPERSION on lines, rings and trees in $O(n)$ time. For rooted trees they provided an algorithm requiring $O(\Delta + \log n)$ bits of memory and $O(D^2)$ rounds and for arbitrary graphs, they provided an algorithm, requiring $O(n \log n)$ bits of memory and $O(m)$ rounds (m is the number of edges in the graph). In [61], a $\Omega(k)$ time lower bound was proved for $k \leq n$. In addition, three deterministic algorithms were provided in [61] for arbitrary graphs. The first algorithm requires $O(k\log\Delta)$ bits of memory and $O(m)$ time, ($\Delta =$ the maximum degree of the graph), the second algorithm requires $O(D \log \Delta)$ bits of memory and $O(\Delta^D)$ time, and the third algorithm requires $O(\log(\max(k, \Delta)))$ bits of memory and $O(mk)$ time. A deterministic algorithm was provided in [62] that runs in $O(\min(m, k\Delta) \log k)$ time and uses $O(\log n)$ bits of memory at each robot. In [64], the problem was studied on grid graphs. The authors presented two deterministic algorithms on anonymous grid graphs that achieve simultaneously optimal bounds with respect to both time and memory complexity. For the first algorithm, the authors considered the usual local communication model where a robot can only communicate with other robots that are present at the same node. Their second algorithm works in global communication model where a robot can communicate with other robots present anywhere on the graph. In the local communication model, they showed that the problem can be solved in an n-node square grid graph in $O(\min(k, \sqrt{n}))$ time with $O(\log k)$ bits of memory at each robot. In the global communication model, the authors showed that it can be solved in $O(\sqrt{k})$ time with $O(\log k)$ bits of memory at each robot. In [63], the authors extended the work in global communication model to arbitrary graphs. They gave three deterministic algorithms, two for arbitrary graphs and one for trees. For arbitrary graphs, their first algorithm is based on DFS traversal and has time complexity of $O(\min(m, k\Delta))$ and memory complexity of $\Theta(\log(\max(k, \Delta)))$. The second algorithm is based on BFS traversal and has time complexity $O(\max(D, k)\Delta(D + \Delta))$ and memory complexity $O(\max(D, \Delta \log k))$. The third algorithm in arbitrary trees is a BFS based algorithm that has time and memory complexity $O(D \max(D, k))$ and $O(\max(D, \Delta \log k))$ respectively. In [94], an algorithm was presented that does not require global knowledge of m, k and Δ as in [62] but still solves the problem by keeping the asymptotically same running time and also with slightly smaller memory space i.e., $O(\log(k + \Delta))$ bits. Recently in [66], as algorithm was presented that solves Dispersion in $O(\min\{m, k\Delta\})$ time with $\Theta(\log(k + \Delta))$ bits of memory at each robot. This is the first algorithm for Dispersion that is optimal in both time and memory in arbitrary anonymous graphs of constant degree, i.e., $\Delta = O(1)$. Furthermore, this result holds in both synchronous and asynchronous settings. In [80], randomization was used to break the $\Omega(\log k)$ memory lower bound for deterministic algorithms. In particular, the authors considered anonymous robots that can generate random bits and gave two deterministic algorithms that achieve dispersion from rooted configurations on an arbitrary graph. The memory complexity of the algorithms are respectively $O(max\{\log \Delta, \log D\})$ and $O(\Delta)$. For arbitrary initial configurations, they gave a random walk based algorithm that requires $O(\log \Delta)$ bits of memory, but the robots do not terminate. In [3], the problem was studied on dynamic rings. Dispersion in arbitrary anonymous dynamic graphs was studied in [65] where authors provided some impossibility, lower and upper bound results. Fault-tolerant Dispersion was considered for the first time in [78] where the authors studied the problem on a ring in presence of Byzantine robots. Byzantine robots on arbitrary anonymous graphs was then considered in [79]. DISPERSION under crash faults was considered in [84]. In [48] the authors investigated the role of communication among co-located robots in achieving dispersion.

The problem of EXPLORATION by mobile robots in static anonymous graph has been studied extensively in the literature [5, 24, 24, 30, 34, 45, 83]. Prior to [71], there have been a few works on EXPLORATION of dynamic graphs, but under assumptions such as complete a priori knowledge of location and timing of topological changes (i.e., *offline* setting) [36,55,57,77] or periodic edges (edges appear periodically) [39,56] or δ-recurrent edges (each edge appears at least once every δ rounds) [57] etc. In the *online* or *live* setting where the location and timing of the changes are unknown, distributed EXPLORATION of graphs without any assumption other than being always connected was first considered in [71]. In particular, they considered the problem on an always connected dynamic ring. They proved that without any knowledge of the size of the ring and without landmark node, EXPLORATION with partial termination is impossible by two robots even if the robots are non-anonymous and have chirality. They also proved that if the robots are anonymous, have no knowledge of size, and there is no landmark node then EXPLORATION with partial termination is impossible by any number of robots even in the presence of chirality. On the positive side the authors showed that under fully synchronous setting, if an upper bound N on the size of the ring is known to two anonymous robots, then EXPLORATION with explicit termination is possible within $3N - 6$ rounds. They then showed that for two anonymous robots, if chirality and a landmark node is present, then exploration with explicit termination is possible within $O(n)$ round, and in the absence of chirality with all other conditions remaining the same, EXPLORATION with explicit termination is possible within $O(n \log n)$ rounds, where n is the size of the ring. They have also proved a number of results in the semi-synchronous setting (i.e., not all robots may be active in each round) under different assumptions. Then in [74], the authors considered robots with unique identifiers and edge crossing detection capability in a ring without any landmark node. They showed that EX-

PLORATION with explicit termination is impossible in the absence of landmark node and the knowledge of n by two robots with access to randomness, even in the presence of chirality, unique identifiers and edge-crossing detection capability. In the absence of randomness even EXPLORATION with partial termination is impossible in the same setting. With three robots under fully synchronous setting, the authors showed that EXPLORATION with explicit termination is possible by three non-anonymous robots with edge-crossing detection capability in absence of any landmark node. Removing the assumption of edge-crossing detection and replacing it with access to randomness, the authors gave a randomized algorithm for EXPLORATION with explicit termination with success probability at least $1 - \frac{1}{n}$. EXPLORATION of an always connected dynamic torus was considered in [51]. In [50] the problem of PERPETUAL EXPLORATION (i.e., every node is to be visited infinitely often) was studied in temporally connected (i.e., may not be always connected but connected over time) graphs. Other problems studied in dynamic graphs include GATHERING [16, 73, 81], DISPERSION [3, 63], PATROLLING [27] etc.

Investigations regarding the computational power of robots under synchronous schedulers was done by the authors Flocchini et. al. in [44]. Main focus of the investigation in this work was which of the two capabilities was more important: *persistent memory* or *communication*. In the course of their investigation they proved that under fully synchronous scheduler communication is more powerful than persistent memory. In addition to that, they gave a complete exhaustive map of the relationships among models and schedulers.

In [17], the previous work of characterizing the relations between the robot models and three type of schedulers was continued. The authors provided a more refined map of the computational landscape for robots operating under fully synchronous and semi-synchronous schedulers, by removing the assumptions on robots' movements of *rigidity* and common *chirality*. Further authors establish some preliminary results with respect to asynchronous scheduler.

The previous two works considered that the robots was assumed to have unlimited amounts of energy. In [18], the authors removed this assumption and started the study of computational capabilities of robots whose energy is limited, albeit renewable. In these systems, the activated entities uses all its energy to execute an LCM cycle and then the energy is restored after a period of inactivity. They studied the impact that memory persistence and communication capabilities have on the computational power of such robots by analyzing the computational relationship between the four models $\{\mathcal{OBLOT}, \mathcal{FSTA}, \mathcal{FCOM}, \mathcal{LUMI}\}$ under the energy constraint. They provided a full characterization of this relationship. Among the many results they proved that for energy-constrained robots, $\mathcal{FCOM}$ is more powerful than $\mathcal{FSTA}$.

In all the three above mentioned works, the robots had full visibility. A robot uses its visibility power in the *Look* phase of the LCM cycle to acquire information about its surroundings, i.e., position and lights (if any) of other robots. The biggest drawback of full visibility assumption is that it is not practically feasible. So, recently some of the authors [7, 41, 49, 87] have considered limited visibility. For example, in [41] they considered that the robots can see up to a fixed radius V from it. So it was important to study the power of different robot models under limited visibility.

In summary, the field of distributed computing by robot swarms encompasses a wide range of problems, from basic gathering and formation tasks to more complex challenges involving memory constraints, synchronization models, and non-trivial spatial environments. Researchers continue to explore and develop algorithms to address these problems in various settings and under different assumptions.

1.3 Overview of the Thesis

The main focus of this thesis is not limited to studying the computational aspects of a single problem, under different model assumptions. Rather the subject matter of this thesis can be interpreted from two broad perspectives. The first is solving a particular problem with minimum number of assumptions, and finding the optimal value of various parameters with which the problems can be solved.

The second is investigating, what affect does various capabilities such as memory, communication, synchronicity have on the problem solving capacity of a robot swarm. Pertaining to the first perspective, in our thesis, we solve the problem of DISPERSION in an arbitrary graph with optimal memory, and we solve the problem of EXPLORATION in dynamic ring, by removing the assumption of landmark node, with minimum number of robots. Pertaining to the second perspective, in our thesis, we investigate what affect variation in the power or capability of *visibility* have on the computational capability of a robot swarm. Here, we also investigate the relation between the capabilities of *visibility* and *synchronicity* and whether limitation in capability can be enhanced by strengthening another capability.

In Chapter 2, we study the DISPERSION problem on an arbitrary connected graph, where the robots are anonymous. Here, we consider that all the robots are located at the same node in the initial configuration. When the robots have identifiers, the leader election process which can be done deterministically, but in our case as the robots are anonymous we take the help of coin-tossing, i.e., the leader election process is probabilistic. We solve the problem with optimal amount of memory. In Chapter 3, we consider the EXPLORATION problem, and to solve it in a dynamic ring without any landmark,i.e., any special node which can be distinguished from other nodes. In this chapter we assume the power of chirality, i.e., all the robots have a common clockwise and anticlockwise direction. We define another problem, MEETING and solve it in the presence of chirality as an essential step to solve the overall problem of EXPLORATION. In Chapter 4, we solve the same problem as Chapter 3 but by removing the assumption of chirality. This changes the whole scenario as solving the problem of MEETING becomes difficult without chirality. Therefore we have to define a new problem called CONTIGUOUS AGREEMENT to solve the problem of MEETING, and eventually EXPLORATION is solved. Then in Chapter 5, we make a comparative analysis of what affect does variation in the *visibility* capability have on the compuatational capability of a robot swarm. Finally in Chapter 6, we discuss some directions for future research.

Chapter 2

Memory Optimal Dispersion by Anonymous Mobile Robots

The DISPERSION problem asks $k \leq n$ robots, initially placed arbitrarily at the nodes of an n-node anonymous graph, to reposition themselves to reach a configuration in which each robot is at a distinct node of the graph.

It is easy to see that the problem cannot be solved deterministically by a set of anonymous robots. Since all robots execute the same deterministic algorithm and initially they are in the same state, the co-located robots will perform the same moves. This is true for each round and hence they will always mirror each other's move and will never do anything different. Hence, throughout the execution of the algorithm, they will stick together and as a result, dispersion cannot be achieved. Using similar arguments, it can be shown that the robots need to have $\Omega(\log k)$ bits of memory each in order to solve the problem by any deterministic algorithm [9]. However, it has been recently shown in [80] that if we consider randomized algorithms, i.e., each robot is given access to a fair coin which can be used to generate random bits, then DISPERSION can be solved by anonymous robots with possibly $o(\log k)$ bits of memory. In [80], the authors gave an algorithm requiring $O(\log \Delta)$ bits of memory. However, in this algorithm, the robots do not terminate. As for terminating algorithms, the authors presented two algorithms for DISPERSION from a *rooted configuration*, i.e., a configuration in which all robots are situated at the same node. The first algorithm requires each robot to have $O(max\{\log \Delta, \log D\})$ bits of memory, where Δ and D are respectively the maximum degree and diameter of G. The second algorithm requires each robot to have $O(\Delta)$ bits of memory. In [80], it is also shown that the robots require $\Omega(\log \Delta)$ bits of memory to achieve dispersion in this setting. Notice that while the memory requirement of the second algorithm is clearly $\omega(\log \Delta)$, that of the first algorithm too can be $\omega(\log \Delta)$ depending on the values of Δ and D. The question of whether the problem can be solved with $O(\log \Delta)$ bits of memory at each robot was left as an open problem. In our work, we answer this question affirmatively by presenting an algorithm with memory complexity $O(\log \Delta)$. The lower bound result presented in [80] implies that the algorithm is asymptotically optimal with respect to memory complexity.

The rest of the chapter is organized as follows. In Section 2.1, some basic definitions and a formal description of the model and the problem are presented. In Section 2.2, we present the main algorithm which solves the problem. In Section 2.3, we the correctness proofs of our main algorithm. In Section 2.4 we finally present the main result obtained.

2.1 Model and Definitions

In this section, we first present a formal description of the model. Next we introduce some definitions and then formally state the problem.

2.1.1 Technical Preliminaries

Graph We consider a connected undirected graph G of n nodes, m edges, diameter D and maximum degree Δ. For any node v, its degree is denoted by $\delta(v)$ or simply δ when there is no ambiguity. The nodes are anonymous, i.e., they do not have any labels. For every edge connected to a node, the node has a corresponding port number for the edge. For every node, the edges incident to the node are uniquely identified by port numbers in the range $[0, \delta - 1]$. There is no relation between the two port numbers of an edge. If u, v are two adjacent nodes then $\text{port}(u, v)$ denotes the port at u that corresponds to the edge between u and v.

Robots Robots are anonymous, i.e., they do not have unique identifiers. The set of all robots in the graph is denoted by $\mathcal{R}$. Each robot has $O(\log \Delta)$ bits of space or memory for computation and to store information. Each robot has a fair coin which they can use to generate random bits. Each robot can communicate with other robots present at the same node by message passing: a robot can broadcast some message which is received by all robots present at the same node. The size of a message is no more than its memory size because it cannot generate a message whose size is greater than its memory size. Therefore, the size of a message must be $O(\log \Delta)$. Also, when there are many robots (co-located at a node) broadcasting their messages, it is not possible for a robot to receive all of these messages due to limited memory. When there is not enough memory to receive all the messages, it receives only a subset of the messages. The view of a robot is local: the only things that a robot can 'see' when it is at some node, are the edges incident to it. The robots have access to the port numbers of these edges. It cannot 'see' the other robots that may be present at the same node. The only way it can detect the presence of other robots is by receiving messages that those robots may broadcast. The robots can move from one node to an adjacent node. Any number of robots are allowed to move via an edge. When a robot moves from a node u to node v, it is aware of the port through which it enters v.

Time Cycle We assume a fully synchronous system. The time progresses in rounds. Each robot knows when a current round ends and when the next round starts. Each round consists of the following.

- A robot first performs a series of synchronous computations and communications. These are called *subrounds*. In each subround, a robot performs some local computations and then broadcasts some messages. The messages received in the ith subround are read in the $(i+1)$th subround. The local computations are based on its memory contents (which contains the messages that it might have received in the last subround and other information that it had stored) and a random bit generated by the fair coin.

- A robot then either remains at the current node or moves through some port.

2.1.2 Problem Statement

A team of k ($\leq n$) robots are initially at the same node of the graph G. The Dispersion problem requires the robots to re-position themselves so that i) there is at most one robot at each node, and ii) all robots have terminated within a finite number of rounds.

2.2 The Algorithm

2.2.1 Local Leader Election

Before presenting our main algorithm, we give a brief description of the LeaderElection() subroutine. We adopt this subroutine from [80]. When $k \geq 1$ robots are co-located together at a node, LeaderElection() subroutine allows exactly one robot to be selected as the leader within one round. Formally, 1) if $k = 1$, the robot finds out that it is the only robot at the node, 2) if $k > 1$, after finitely many subrounds (with high probability [1]), i) exactly one robot is elected as leader, ii) all robots can detect when the process is completed. Each robot starts off as a candidate for leader. In the first subround, every robot broadcasts 'start'. If a robot finds that it has received no message, it then concludes that it is the only robot at the node. Otherwise, it concludes that there are multiple robots at the node and does the following. In each subsequent subround, each candidate flips a fair coin. If heads, it broadcasts 'heads', otherwise it does not broadcast anything. If a robot gets tails, and receives at least one ('heads') message, it

[1] Throughout we use "high probability" to mean probabilty at least $1 - k^{-c}$, where $c \geq 1$

stops being a candidate. This process is repeated until exactly one robot, say r, broadcasts in a given subround. In this subround, r broadcasts 'heads', but receives no message, while all other non-candidate robots have not broadcasted, but received exactly one message. So r elects itself as the leader, and all robots detect that the process is completed. The process requires $O(1)$ bits of memory at each robot and terminates in $O(\log k)$ subrounds with high probability.

2.2.2 Overview of the Algorithm

In this subsection, we present a brief overview of the algorithm. The execution of our algorithm can be divided into three stages. In the first stage, the robots, together as a group, perform a DFS traversal in the search of empty nodes, starting from the node where they are placed together initially. We shall call this node the *root* and denote it by v_R. Whenever the group reaches an empty node, they perform the LEADERELECTION() subroutine to elect a leader. The leader settles at that node, while the rest of the group continues the DFS traversal. Note that the settled robot does not terminate. This is because when the robots that are performing the DFS return to that node, they need to detect that the node is occupied by a settled robot. Recall that a robot cannot distinguish between an empty node and a node with a terminated robot. Therefore, the active settled robot helps the travelling robots to distinguish between an occupied node and an empty node, and also provides them with other information that is required to correctly execute the DFS. The size of the travelling group decreases by one, each time the DFS traversal reaches an empty node. The first stage completes when each robot has found an empty node for itself. Let r_L denote the last robot that finds an empty node, v_L, for itself. Although dispersion is achieved, this robot will not terminate. The other settled robots do not know that dispersion is achieved and will remain active. Therefore r_L needs to revisit those nodes and ask the settled robots to terminate. First r_L will return to the root v_R via the *rootpath* which is the unique path in the DFS tree from v_L to v_R. This is the second stage of the algorithm. In the third stage, r_L performs a second DFS traversal and asks the active settled robots to terminate. Since the active settled robots play

Variable	Description
role	It indicates the role that the robot is playing in the algorithm. It takes values from {`explore`, `settled`, `return`, `acknowledge`, `done`}. Initially, *role* $\leftarrow$ `explore`.
entered	It indicates the port through which the robot has entered the current node. Initially, *entered* $\leftarrow \emptyset$. For simplicity, assume that it is automatically updated when the robot entered a node.
received	It indicates the message(s) received by the robot in the current subround. After the end of each subround, the messages are erased, i.e., it is reset to $\emptyset$. Initially, *received* $\leftarrow \emptyset$.
direction	It indicates the direction of movement of a robot during a DFS traversal. It takes values from {`forward`, `backward`}. Initially, *direction* $\leftarrow$ `forward`.
parent	For a settled robot on some node, it indicates the port number towards the parent of that node in the DFS tree. Initially, *parent* $\leftarrow \emptyset$.
child	For a settled robot on some node that is on the rootpath, it indicates the port number towards the child of that node in the DFS tree that is on the rootpath. Initially, *child* $\leftarrow \emptyset$.
visited	For a settled robot on some node, it indicates whether the node where the robot is settled has been visited by r_L in the third stage. Initially, *visited* $\leftarrow 0$.

Table 2.1: Description of the variables used by the robots

a crucial role in the DFS traversal, r_L needs to be careful about the order in which it should ask the settled robots to terminate. Finally, r_L terminates after it returns to v_L.

A pseudocode description of the algorithm is given in Algorithm 1. In Table 2.1, we give details of the variables used by the robots. If *variable_name* is some variable, then we shall denote the value of the variable stored by r as $r.variable\_name$.

Algorithm 1: Dispersion

```
Procedure DISPERSION()
    r ← myself
    if r.role = settled then
        SETTLED()                                   // Algorithm 2
    else if r.role = explore then
        EXPLORE()                                   // Algorithm 3
    else if r.role = return then
        RETURN()                                    // Algorithm 4
    else if r.role = acknowledge then
        ACKNOWLEDGE()                               // Algorithm 5
    else if r.role = done then
        TERMINATE()
```

Algorithm 2: Algorithm for role settled

```
Procedure SETTLED()
    if I am queried then
        BROADCAST(role = settled, parent = r.parent, child = r.child, visited = r.visited)
    else if r.received = "Set child x" then
        r.child ← x
    else if r.received = "Set visited = 1" then
        r.visited ← 1
    else if r.received = "terminate" then
        TERMINATE()
```

Algorithm 3: Algorithm for role explore

```
Procedure EXPLORE()
    QUERY()
    if r.received = ∅ then
        LEADERELECTION()
        if I am alone then
            r.role ← return
            Move through r.entered
        else if I am elected as leader then
            r.role ← settled
            r.parent ← r.entered
        else if I am not elected as leader then
            if r.entered = ∅ then
                Move via port 0
            else
                if (r.entered + 1 = r.entered) mod δ then
                    r.direction ← backward
                Move via port (r.entered + 1) mod δ
    else if r.received = "role = settled, parent = x, child = ∅, visited = 0" then
        if r.direction = forward then
            r.direction ← backward
            Move via port r.entered
        else if r.direction = backward then
            if (r.entered + 1) mod δ = x then
                Move via port (r.entered + 1) mod δ
            else
                r.direction ← forward
                Move via port (r.entered + 1) mod δ
```

Algorithm 4: Algorithm for role return

```
Procedure RETURN()
    QUERY()
    if r.received = "role = settled, parent = x, child = ∅, visited = 0" then
        if x ≠ ∅ then
            BROADCAST("Set child r.entered")
            Move via port x
        else
            BROADCAST("Set child r.entered")
            r.direction ← forward
            r.role ← acknowledge
            r.entered ← ∅
```

Algorithm 5: Algorithm for role acknowledge

```
Procedure ACKNOWLEDGE()
    QUERY()
    if r.received = "role = settled, parent = x, child = y, visited = 0" then
        BROADCAST("Set visited = 1")
        if r.entered = ∅ then
            Move via port 0
        else
            if r.entered = (r.entered + 1) mod δ then
                r.direction ← backward
                BROADCAST("terminate")
            else if y = (r.entered + 1) mod δ then
                BROADCAST("terminate")
            Move via port (r.entered + 1) mod δ
    else if r.received = "role = settled, parent = x, child = y, visited = 1" then
        if r.direction = forward then
            r.direction ← backward
            Move via port r.entered
        else if r.direction = backward then
            if x = (r.entered + 1) mod δ then
                BROADCAST("terminate")
            else if y = (r.entered + 1) mod δ then
                r.direction ← forward
                BROADCAST("terminate")
            else
                r.direction ← forward
            Move via port (r.entered + 1) mod δ
    else if r.received = ∅ then
        if r.direction = forward then
            r.direction ← backward
        else if r.direction = backward then
            r.role = done
        Move via port r.entered
```

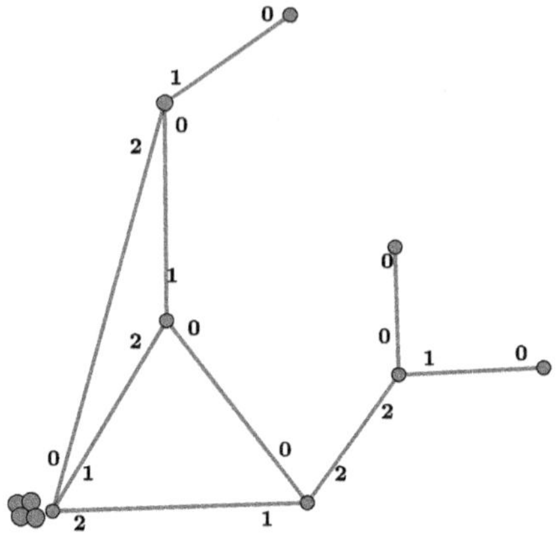

Figure 2.1: Configuration at the start of the Algorithm

2.2.3 Detailed Description of the Algorithm

In the starting configuration, all robots are present at a single node, refer to Figure 2.1. We call this node the root node and denote it by v_R. Initially, *role* of each robot is `explore`. In the first stage, the robots have to perform a DFS traversal together as a group. This group of robots is called the *exploring group*, refer to Figure 2.2.

Whenever the exploring group reaches an empty node (a node with no settled robot), one of the robots will settle at that node, i.e., it will change its *role* to `settled` and remain at that node. For the rest of the algorithm, it does not move. However, it stays active and checks for any received messages. A settled robot can receive three types of messages as the following:

- it may receive a query about the contents of its internal memory
- it may receive an instruction to change the value of some variable
- it may be asked to terminate

When queried about its memory, it broadcasts a message containing its *role*,

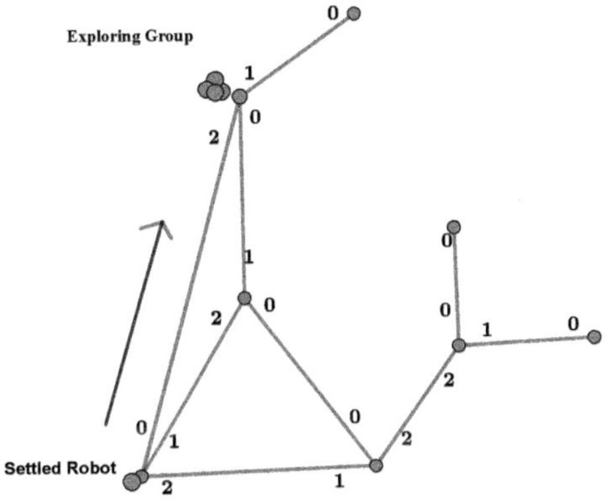

Figure 2.2: The Exploring Group

parent, *child* and *visited*. If it is asked to change the value of some variable or terminate, then it does so accordingly. Any robot with role `explore`, `return` or `acknowledge`, in the first subround of any round, broadcasts a message querying about internal memory of any settled robot at the node. If it receives no message in the second subround, then it concludes that there is no settled robot at that node. Whenever the robots find that there is no settled robot at the node, during the first stage, they start the LEADERELECTION() subroutine to elect a leader. For any robot r, LEADERELECTION() results in one of the following outcomes:

- it is elected as the leader
- it is not elected as the leader
- it finds that it is the only robot at that node

In the first case, it changes $r.role$ to `settled` and sets $r.parent$ equal to $r.entered$. Recall that $r.entered$ is the port through which it entered the current node and in the beginning, $r.entered$ is set to $\emptyset$. We shall call $r.parent$ the *parent port* of the node where r resides. We shall refer to a robot that has set its *role* to `settled` as a *settled robot*. In the second case, it will continue the DFS: if $r.entered = \emptyset$, it leaves via port 0 and if $r.entered \neq \emptyset$, it leaves via port $(r.entered + 1) \bmod \delta$. If

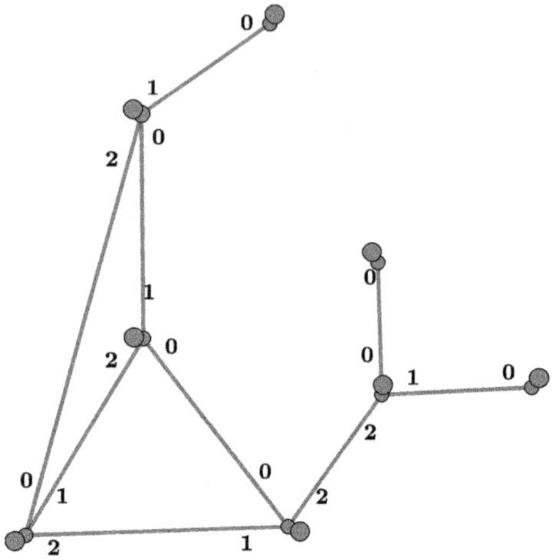

Figure 2.3: The Configuration at the end of the first stage

$(r.entered + 1) = r.entered \bmod \delta$, it changes its variable *direction* to `backward` before exiting the node. Recall that the variable *direction* is used to indicate the direction of the movement during a DFS traversal. In the third case, it changes *r.role* to `return`.

Now consider the case where the robots find that there is a settled robot at the node. If the *direction* is set to `forward` when they encounter the settled robot, it indicates the onset of a cycle. So the robots change the *direction* to `backward` and leave the node via the port through which they entered it. Now suppose that the *direction* is set to `backward` when they encounter the settled robot. Recall that the robots have received from the settled robot, say a, a message which contains *a.parent*. The robots check if *a.parent* is equal to the port number through which it entered, say z, plus 1 (modulo the degree of the node). If yes, it implies that the robots have moved through all edges adjacent to the node, and hence they leave the node via *a.parent* which is the port through which they entered for the first time. If no, then it means that they have not moved through the port $(z+1)$ mod δ before. So they change the direction to `forward` and leave via $(z+1)$ mod δ.

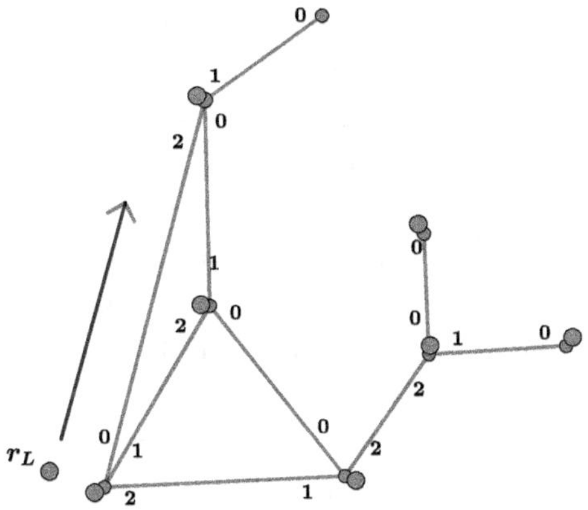

Figure 2.4: The Configuration at the beginning of the third stage

The DFS traversal in the first stage ends when a robot, say r_L, with *role* set to `explore`, finds that it is the only robot at a node, say v_L. Recall that when this happens, r_L changes its *role* to `return`. At this point, the first stage ends, and the second stage starts, refer to Figure 2.3. It then leaves v_L via the port through which it entered. In each of the following rounds where the *role* of r_L is `return`, it does the following. In the first subround, it broadcasts a query. In the next subround, it receives a message from the settled robot at that node which contains its *parent*. If the obtained value of *parent*, say x, is not $\emptyset$, it means that r_L is yet to reach the root v_R. Then r_L broadcasts an instruction for the settled robot to change the value of its *child* to the port via which r_L entered the node. This value of *child* will be called the *child port* of the node. After broadcasting the instruction, r_L leaves through the port x. If $x = \emptyset$, then it means that r_L has reached the root v_R. In this case, r_L broadcasts the same instruction and then changes the values of r_L.*role*, r_L.*direction* and r_L.*entered* to respectively `acknowledge`, `forward` and $\emptyset$. At this point the second stage ends, and the third stage starts, refer to Figure 2.4.

In the following rounds, r_L with *role* `acknowledge` does the following. In the first subround, it broadcasts a query. It either receives a reply or does not. If it receives a message, then it contains the values of *parent*, say x, and *child*, say y, and *visited* of the settled robot at that node. Now, the value of variable *visited* can be 0 or 1. If the value of *visited* is 0, it denotes that the settled robot is visited for the first time in the third stage. Then in the next subround, the robot r_L then broadcasts a message instructing the settled robot to change the value of its variable *visited* to 1. Now $(r_L.entered + 1) \bmod \delta$ can be equal to $r_L.entered$ (the case of one degree node) or y or neither of them. In the former case, it changes its variable *direction* to `backward`. In the first two cases, it broadcasts a message instructing the settled robot to terminate and leaves through port $(r_L.entered + 1) \bmod \delta$. If $(r_L.entered + 1) \bmod \delta$ is neither equal to $r_L.entered$, nor equal to y, r_L just exits through $(r_L.entered + 1) \bmod \delta$ without broadcasting any message for termination. If the value of *visited* is 1, it denotes that the settled robot has been visited before in the third stage. If the value of variable *direction* of r_L is `forward`, it changes the value of *direction* to `backward` and exits through the port through which it entered the node at the previous round. Otherwise the value of variable *direction* of r_L is `backward`. In this case, three sub-cases arise. If $(r_L.entered + 1) \bmod \delta$ is equal to x, then r_L broadcasts a message instructing the settled robot to terminate, and then r_L exits through the port $(r_L.entered + 1) \bmod \delta$. Otherwise if, $(r_L.entered + 1) \bmod \delta$ is equal to y, then also r_L broadcasts a message instructing the settled robot to terminate, changes the variable *direction* to `forward` and then r_L exits through the port $(r_L.entered + 1) \bmod \delta$. If $(r_L.entered + 1) \bmod \delta$ is neither equal to x, nor y, then r_L changes *direction* to `forward` and exits through $(r_L.entered + 1) \bmod \delta$. Now, we consider the case where r_L in third stage does not receive any answer to its query. If its *direction* is set to `forward`, it changes its *direction* to `backward` and then exits through the same port by which it entered the node in the previous round. If its direction is set to `backward`, then it means that r_L was at v_L in the previous round. So r_L changes its *role* to `done` and leaves the node through the port via which it entered. Then it will reach v_L in the next round and it will find that its *role* is `done` and terminate, refer to Figure 2.5.

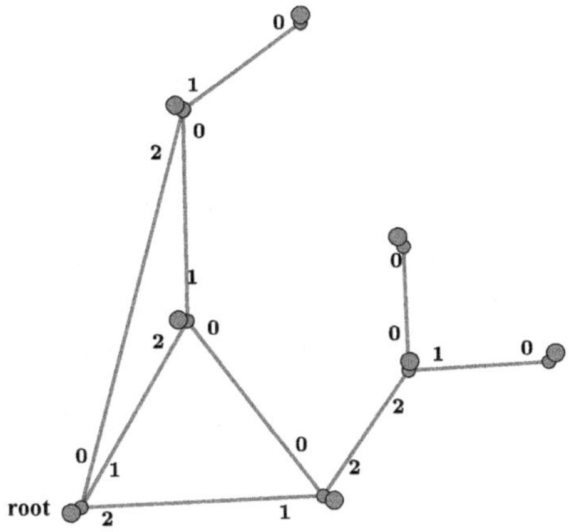

Figure 2.5: Configuration at the end of the third stage. The red colour indicates that all the robots have terminated.

2.3 Correctness proof and Complexity Analysis

The first stage of our algorithm is the same as that of [80]. The robots simply perform a DFS traversal. Whenever a new node is visited, one of the robots settles there. The DFS continues until k distinct nodes are visited. To see that the DFS traversal can be correctly executed in our setting, it suffices to verify that the robots can correctly ascertain 1) if a node is previously visited and 2) if all neighbors of a node have been visited. For 1), observe that the presence of settled robot at a node indicates that the node has already been visited. So, when the robots with *direction* `forward` go to a node which has a settled robot, it backtracks, i.e., it changes its *direction* to `backward` and leaves the node via the port through which it had entered. For 2), observe that the port p through which robots first enter a node v is set as its parent port, i.e., the robot settled at v sets its variable *parent* to p. Then the robots will move through all other ports with *direction* `forward` in the order $p+1, p+2, \ldots, \delta-1, 0, 1, \ldots, p-1$ (unless the DFS is stopped midway for k distinct nodes have been visited). This is because if the robots leaves via a port q (with *direction* `forward`), it re-enters v

via the same port q after some rounds (with *direction* `backward`) and then leaves via $(q+1) \bmod \delta(v)$ (with *direction* `forward`) in the next round if $(q+1) \bmod \delta(v) \neq p$. Clearly, when $(q+1) \bmod \delta(v) = p$, it indicates that the robots have moved through all ports other than p with *direction* `forward`, i.e., all neighbors of v have been visited. The robots can check if $(q+1) \bmod \delta(v) = p$ because their variable *entered* is equal to q and the variable *parent* of the robot settled at v is equal to p. Inspecting the pseudocodes, it is easy to see that these are correctly implemented in the algorithm. Therefore we have the following result.

Lemma 2.1. *There is a round t_1, at the beginning of which*

1. *each node of G has at most one robot*
2. role *of exactly one robot r_L is* ***explore*** *and the role of the remaining $k-1$ robots is* ***settled***
3. *if $V' \subseteq V$ is the set of nodes occupied by robots, then $G[V']$ (the subgraph of G induced by V') is connected*
4. *if $E' \subseteq E$ is the set of edges corresponding to the variable* parent *of robots in $\mathcal{R} \setminus \{r_L\}$ and variable* entered *of r_L, then the graph $T = T(V', E')$ is a DFS spanning tree of $G[V']$,*
5. *r_L is at a leaf node v_L of T.*

In the following lemmas, we present some observations regarding the execution of DFS traversal in the first stage.

Observation 2.1. *If v is a non-rootpath node, then the exploring group leaves it via its parent port once. If v is a rootpath node other than v_L, then the exploring group leaves it via its child port once.*

Observation 2.2. *Suppose that v is a non-rootpath node and the exploring group leaves v through its parent port at round t with direction* ***backward***. *If the exploring group returns to v at some round $t', t < t' \leq t_1$, then its direction must be* ***forward***.

Observation 2.3. *Suppose that v is a rootpath node and the exploring group leaves v through its child port at round t with direction* $\texttt{forward}$*. If the exploring group returns to v at some round $t', t < t' \leq t_1$, then its direction must be* $\texttt{forward}$*.*

There is a unique path, i.e., the rootpath $v_R = v_1, v_2, \ldots, v_s = v_L$ in $T(V', E')$ from v_R to v_L. Furthermore, for any consecutive vertices v_i, v_{i+1} on the path 1) if $i + 1 < s$, the variable *parent* of the settled robot at v_{i+1} is set to $\text{port}(v_{i+1}, v_i)$ and 2) if $i + 1 = s$, the variable *entered* of robot r_L at v_{i+1} is set to $\text{port}(v_{i+1}, v_i)$. So, according to our algorithm, r_L will move along this path to reach v_R. For each node $v_i, i < s$, on the rootpath, when r_L reaches v_i along its way to v_R, it instructs the settled robot at v_i to set its variable *child* to $\text{port}(v_i, v_{i+1})$. Therefore, we have the following result.

Lemma 2.2. *There is a round t_2, at the beginning of which*

1. *r_L is at v_R with $r_L.role =$* $\texttt{return}$
2. *each node of $T(V', E') \setminus \{v_L\}$ has a settled robot*
3. *if $v_R = v_1, v_2, \ldots, v_s = v_L$ is the rootpath and r_i is the settled robot at $v_i, i < s$, then $r_i.child = port(v_i, v_{i+1})$*
4. *if r is a settled robot on a non-rootpath node, then $r.child = \emptyset$*

From round $t_2 + 1$, r_L will start a second DFS traversal. This DFS traversal is trickier than the earlier one because the settled robots will one by one terminate during the process. Recall that the settled robots played an important role in the first DFS. We shall prove that r_L will correctly execute the second DFS traversal. In fact, we shall prove that the DFS traversal in the first stage is exactly same as the DFS traversal in the third stage in the sense that if the exploring group is at node v at round $i < t_1$ (in the first stage), then r_L is at node v at round $t_2 + i$ (in the third stage).

Let us first introduce a definition. In the following definition, whenever we say 'at round', it is to be understood as 'at the beginning of round'. Round i in the first stage is said to be *identical* to round j in the third stage if the exploring group at round i and r_L at round j are at the same node, say u and one of the following holds:

I1 At round i, there is no settled robot at u, the exploring group contains more than one robot and the variable *direction* for each robot in the exploring group is set to `forward`. At round j there is a settled robot at u with its variable *visited* set to 0. The variables *direction* and *entered* of r_L at round j are equal to those of each robot in the exploring group at round i.

I2 At round i, there is a settled robot at u, the variable *direction* for each robot in the exploring group is set to `forward` and the variable *entered* for each robot in the exploring group is $\neq \emptyset$. At round j, either there is a terminated robot at u, or there is a settled robot at u with its variable *visited* set to 1. The variables *direction* and *entered* of r_L at round j are equal to those of each robot in the exploring group at round i .

I3 At round i, there is a settled robot at u, the variable *direction* for each robot in the exploring group is set to `backward` and the variable *entered* for each robot in the exploring group is $\neq \emptyset$. At round j, there is an active settled robot at u with its variable *visited* set to 1. The variables *direction* and *entered* of r_L at round j are equal to those of each robot in the exploring group at round i .

Lemma 2.3. *Round i is identical to* $t_2 + i$ *for all* $1 \leq i < t_1$.

Proof. We prove this by induction. At the beginning of round 1, the exploring group (consisting of more than one robot) is at the root node v_R, there is no settled robot at v_R, and the variables *direction* and *entered* of each robot in the exploring group are set to `forward` and $\emptyset$ respectively. Note that when the robot r_L enters the root node v_R at round t_2, it sets its *direction* and *entered* to `forward` and $\emptyset$ respectively, and does not move (See line 8-11 in Algorithm 1). Hence at the beginning of round $t_2 + 1$, r_L is at node v_R, with its *direction* and *entered* set to `forward` and $\emptyset$ respectively. Furthermore, there is a settled robot at v_R at round t_2+1. This is the robot which was elected as the leader in round 1 and had settled there. Since the variable *visited* of this robot was initially set to 0 and it has been not instructed to change it thus far, it is still set to 0 at the beginning of t_2+1. These observations imply that I1 holds and round 1 is identical to t_2+1.

Now assume that round j is identical to round t_2+j for all $1 \leq j \leq i-1, i < t_1$. We shall prove that round i is identical to round t_2+i. Let the robot r_L be at node u at round t_2+i-1. Then it implies that the exploring group was at node u at round $i-1$. Now we can have following three cases.

Case 1. Suppose that at round $i-1$, 1) there is no settled robot at u, 2) the exploring group contains more than one robot and 3) the variable *direction* for each robot in the exploring group is set to `forward`. Suppose that their variable *entered* are set to p. Then the robots will perform the LEADERELECTION() protocol and one of them will settle. The remaining robots will move via 0 if $p=\emptyset$ or otherwise, will move via $(p+1) \bmod \delta$. In the later case, the robots will change their *direction* to `backward` iff $(p+1) \bmod \delta = p$. Since we assumed that round $i-1$ is identical to round t_2+i-1, at the beginning of round t_2+i-1, 1) r_L is at u, 2) there is a settled robot at u with its variable *visited* set to 0, and 3) the variables *direction* and *entered* of r_L are equal to `forward` and p. According to our algorithm, r_L will move via 0 if $p=\emptyset$ or otherwise, will move via $(p+1)$ mod δ. In the later case, r_L will change its *direction* to `backward` iff $(p+1)$ mod $\delta = p \Leftrightarrow \delta(u) = 1$. Hence the exploring group at round i and r_L at t_2+i must be at the same node, say v, and have same values of *direction* and *entered*. So now it remains to show that one of I1, I2 or I3 is true for round i and t_2+i. For this, consider the following two cases.

Case 1a. First consider the case where the exploring group and r_L exit u with *direction* `forward` at round $i-1$ and t_2+i-1 respectively. At the beginning of round i, the exploring group has more than one robots as $i<t_1$. Now, at the beginning of round i, v either has no settled robot or has a settled robot. In the first case, it implies that exploring group is entering v for the first time at round

i. The robots will then perform the LEADERELECTION() protocol and one of them, say a, will settle. By the induction hypothesis, it implies that r_L will enter v for the first time in the third stage at round $t_2 + i$. Hence the settled robot a must be there with the value of *visited* set to 0. So I1 holds and hence round i is identical to round $t_2 + i$. In the second case, it implies that the exploring group had entered v at some previous round $j < i$. Then by the induction hypothesis, r_L had visited v at round $t_2 + j < t_2 + i$. Hence, if the robot a is active, then variable *visited* of a is 1, or otherwise a has terminated. So I2 holds and hence round i is identical to round $t_2 + i$.

Case 1b. Now consider the case where the exploring group and r_L exit u with *direction* `backward` at round $i - 1$ and $t_2 + i - 1$ respectively. This implies that u is a one degree node. Also, the exploring group and r_L were at v at round $i - 2$ and $t_2 + i - 2$ respectively. Therefore, there must be a settled robot, say b, present at v , when the exploring group visits it at round i, as the node was visited earlier. So when r_L enters v at round $t_2 + i$, if b is still active, its *visited* value is set to 1 and I3 holds. We prove that this is the only case. For the sake of contradiction, let us assume that b has terminated. Consider the following cases.

- First let v be a non-rootpath node. Since b has terminated, it implies that r_L had exited v via its parent port with *direction* `backward` at some round $t_2 + l < t_2 + i - 1$. Then by the induction hypothesis, the exploring group exited v via its parent port with *direction* `backward` at some round $l < i - 1$. But then the fact that the exploring group returns to v with *direction* `backward` at round i contradicts Observation 2.2.

- Now let v be a rootpath node. Since b has terminated, it implies that r_L had exited v via its child port with *direction* `forward` at some round $t_2 + l < t_2 + i - 1$. Then by the induction hypothesis, the exploring group exited v via its child port with *direction* `forward` at some round $l < i - 1$. But then the fact that the exploring group returns to v with *direction* `backward` at round i contradicts Observation 2.3.

Case 2. At the beginning of round $i - 1$, 1) there is a settled robot at u, 2) the variable *direction* for each robot in the exploring group is set to `forward` and 3) the variable *entered* for each robot in the exploring group is $p \neq \emptyset$. According to our algorithm, the exploring group will change their *direction* to `backward` and leave the node via p. Since we assumed that round $i-1$ is identical to round t_2+i-1, at the beginning of round t_2+i-1, r_L is at u, there is either an active settled robot at u with its variable *visited* set to 1 or a terminated robot, and the variables *direction* and *entered* of r_L are equal to `forward` and p respectively. According to our algorithm, r_L will change it *direction* to `backward` and leave the node via p. Hence the exploring group at round i and r_L at t_2+i must be at the same node, say v, both having *direction* set to `backward` and *entered* set to $\text{port}(v, u)$.

It is clear that the exploring group and r_L was at v at rounds $i-2$ and t_2+i-2 respectively. Hence, there is a settled robot at v, say a, at round i, as it had been visited at least once before. Also, a is still situated at v at round t_2+i, either active or terminated. If it is active, then the value of its variable *visited* is 1, as r_L had been at v at round t_2+i-2. So, in this case I3 holds. Using the same arguments as in Case 1b, we can show that this is the only possible case.

Case 3. At the beginning of round $i-1$, 1) there is a settled robot at u, say a, 2) the variable *direction* for each robot in the exploring group is set to `backward` and 3) the variable *entered* for each robot in the exploring group is $p \neq \emptyset$. Let the *parent* of a be equal to x. According to our algorithm, the robots will not change their *direction* if $(p+1) \bmod \delta = x$ (Case 3a), and otherwise, it will change it to `forward` (Case 3b). In any case, they will leave the node via port $(p+1) \bmod \delta$. Since we assumed that round $i-1$ is identical to round t_2+i-1, at the beginning of round t_2+i-1, 1) r_L is at u, 2) there is a settled robot at u with its variable *visited* set to 1, and 3) the variables *direction* and *entered* of r_L are equal to `backward` and p respectively. Since a settled robot does not move or change its *parent*, the settled robot at u at round t_2+i-1 is a and its *parent* is set to x. According to our algorithm, r_L will not change its *direction* if $(p+1) \bmod \delta = x$ (Case 3a), and otherwise, it will change it to `forward` (Case 3b). In any case, they will leave the node via port $(p+1) \bmod \delta$. Hence at round i and

$t_2 + i$, the exploring group and r_L must be at the same node, say v, with same *direction* and *entered*. So now it remains to show that one of I1, I2 or I3 is true for round i and $t_2 + i$.

Case 3a. Clearly in this case v must have been visited at least once before round i in the first stage. Hence a robot, say c, is already settled there at round i. Hence, at round $t_2 + i$, either c is active with *visited* set to 1, or is terminated. In the first case, I3 holds and hence we are done. We can prove that the later case is impossible using the same arguments as in Case 1b.

Case 3b. If there is no settled robot at v at round i, then the exploring group is visiting v for the first time and one of them, say b, will settle there. It implies from our induction hypothesis that r_L is also visiting v for the first time in the third stage at round $t_2 + i$. Hence it will find b with its *visited* set to 0. So I1 holds. If there is a settled robot at v at round i, say c, then at round $t_2 + i$, v has c which is either terminated or its variable *visited* set to 1. So we see that I2 holds.

□

Lemma 2.4. *By round $t_2 + t_1$ all the settled robots have terminated.*

Proof. A settled robot at a non-rootpath node will terminate if r_L moves from that node to its parent and a settled robot at a rootpath node will terminate if r_L moves from that node to its child. So the result follows from Observation 2.1 and Lemma 2.3. □

Lemma 2.5. *At round $t_2 + t_1 + 2$, r_L terminates at v_L.*

Proof. It follows from Lemma 2.3 that r_L will be at v_{s-1} at round $t_2 + t_1 - 1$. It is easy to see that it will then move to $v_s = v_L$ with *direction* `forward`. So at round $t_2 + t_1$, r_L is at v_L with *direction* set to `forward`. Since v_L has no settled robot, r_L will change its *direction* to `backward` and exit through the port through which it entered v_L. But moving through this port leads to v_{s-1}. The settled robot at this node is already terminated by Lemma 2.4. Hence at round $t_2 + t_1 + 1$, r_L enters with *direction* `backward` a node where it does not receive any message. So it will then change its *role* to `done` and exit the port through which it entered the node. Therefore, at round $t_2 + t_1 + 2$, r_l again returns to v_L, this time with *role* `done`, and hence will terminate. □

Lemma 2.6. *Algorithm 1 is correct.*

Proof. It follows from the above results that at round t_2+t_1+2, dispersion accomplished and all robots have terminated. Hence Algorithm 1 solves DISPERSION from any rooted configuration. □

2.4 The Main Result

Lemma 2.7. *Algorithm 1 requires $O(\log \Delta)$ bits of memory at each robot and this is optimal in terms of memory complexity.*

Proof. The LEADERELECTION() subroutine costs $O(1)$ bits of memory for each robot. Among the variables, *role*, *visited* and *direction* costs $O(1)$ bits of memory, and the variables *entered*, *parent*, *child*, *received* costs $O(\log \Delta)$ bits of memory for each robot. Hence the algorithm requires $O(\log \Delta)$ bits of memory at each robot. The optimality follows from the lower bound result proved in [80]. □

Lemma 2.8. *Algorithm 1 requires $\Theta(k^2)$ rounds in the worst case.*

Proof. Exactly k distinct nodes are visited in our algorithm. In the first stage, movement of the exploring group takes $O(m')$ rounds where m' is the number of edges in the subgraph of G induced by these k vertices. Clearly $m' = O(k^2)$. So the first stage requires $O(k^2)$ rounds. The third stage requires (k^2) rounds as well since apart from the last two rounds, it is exactly identical to the first stage. Clearly the second round takes $O(k)$ rounds. So the overall round complexity is $O(k^2)$.

To see that $\Omega(k^2)$ rounds may be required, consider the graph of size k in Fig. 2.6. Here $\text{port}(v_R, v_1) = 0$, $\text{port}(v_1, v_R) = 0$, $\text{port}(v_1, v_2) = 1$, $\text{port}(v_1, v_L) = 2$.

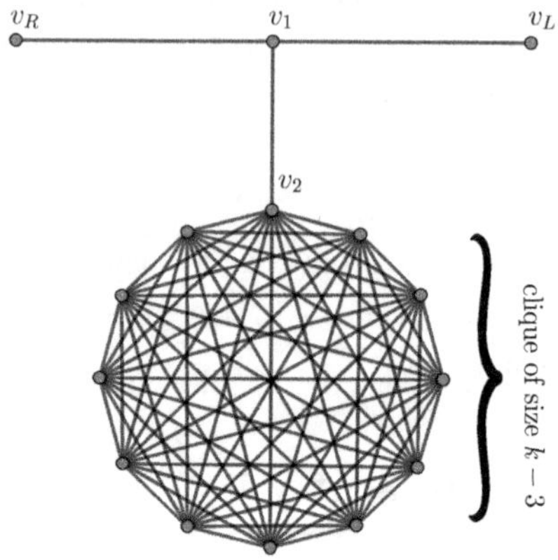

Figure 2.6: An example where Algorithm 1 requires $\Theta(k^2)$ rounds to complete.

Here, after reaching v_1, the exploring group will go v_2. It is easy to see that $\Theta(k^2)$ rounds will be spent inside the $(k-3)-$clique. Finally the last robot will return to v_1 and then move to v_L. □

Hence we establish the following result.

Theorem 2.1. *The* Dispersion *problem can be solved with $O(\log \Delta)$ bits of memory at each robot (which is optimal in terms of memory complexity) and $\Theta(k^2)$ rounds in the worst case.*

2.5 Concluding Remarks

In this chapter, we have presented a memory optimal randomized algorithm for Dispersion from rooted configuration by anonymous robots. This resolves an open problem posed in [80]. Time complexity of our algorithm is $\Theta(k^2)$ rounds in the worst case. Any algorithm that solves the problem requires $\Omega(k)$ rounds in the worst case. To see this, consider a path with $n \geq k$ nodes with all robots initially at one of its one degree nodes. An interesting open problem is to close this gap.

For arbitrary configurations, the random walk based algorithm presented in [80] requires the robots to stay active indefinitely. Therefore an interesting open question is whether it is possible to solve the problem by anonymous robots from non-rooted configurations without requiring robots to stay active indefinitely.

Chapter 3

Exploring a Dynamic Ring without Landmark, with Chirality

In Chapter 2, we studied the DISPERSION problem, and gave an algorithm which was optimum in terms of memory complexity when the robots considered were anonymous. In this Chapter we study the EXPLORATION problem, which is another relevant problem to understand the power of a robot swarm in graph topology.

Consider a team of robots located at the nodes of a graph. The robots are able to move from a node to any neighboring node. The EXPLORATION problem asks for a distributed algorithm that allows the robots to explore the graph, with the requirement that each node has to be visited by at least one robot. Being one of the fundamental problems in the field of autonomous multi-robot systems, the problem has been extensively studied in the literature. However, the majority of existing literature studies the problem for *static* graphs, i.e., the topology of the graph does not change over time. Recently within the distributed computing community, there has been a surge of interest in highly dynamic graphs: the topology of the graph changes continuously and unpredictably. In highly dynamic graphs, the topological changes are not seen as occasional anomalies (e.g., link failures, congestion, etc), but rather integral part of the nature of the system

[67, 89]. We refer the readers to [20] for a compendium of different models of dynamic networks considered in the literature. If time is discrete, i.e., changes occur in rounds, then the evolution of a dynamic graph can be seen as a sequence of static graphs. A popular assumption in this context is *always connected* (Class 9 of [20]), i.e., the graph is connected in each round.

In the dynamic setting, the EXPLORATION problem was first studied in [71]. In particular, the authors studied the EXPLORATION problem in a dynamic but always connected ring by a set of autonomous robots. They showed that EXPLORATION is solvable by two anonymous robots (robots do not have unique identifiers) under fully synchronous setting (i.e., all robots are active in each round) if there is a single observably different node in the ring called *landmark* node. They also proved that in absence of a landmark node, two robots cannot solve EXPLORATION even if the robots are non-anonymous and they have chirality, i.e., they agree on clockwise and counterclockwise orientation of the ring. The impossibility result holds even if we relax the problem to EXPLORATION with partial termination. As opposed to the standard explicit termination setting where all robots are required to terminate, in the partial termination setting at least one robot is required to detect exploration and terminate. If the robots are anonymous, then EXPLORATION with partial termination with chirality remains unsolvable in absence of a landmark node even with arbitrary number of robots. Then in [74], the authors considered the EXPLORATION problem (without chirality and requiring explicit termination) with no landmark node. Since the problem cannot be solved even with arbitrary number of anonymous robots, they considered non-anonymous robots, in particular, robots with unique identifiers. Since the problem is unsolvable by two non-anonymous robots, they considered the question that whether the problem can be solved by three non-anonymous robots. They showed that the answer is yes if the robots are endowed with edge crossing detection capability. Edge crossing detection capability is a strong assumption which enables two robots moving in opposite directions through an edge in the same round to detect each other and also exchange information. In collaborative tasks like exploration, the robots are often required to meet at a node and exchange information. However, the edge crossing detection capability allows two robots to exchange information even without meeting at a node. The assumption is particularly helpful when the robots do not have chirality where it is more difficult to ensure meeting. Even if we do not allow exchange of information, simple detection of the swap can be useful in deducing important information about the progress of an algorithm. In [74], it was also shown that the assumption of edge crossing detection can be removed with the help of randomness. In particular, without assuming edge crossing detection capability, they gave a randomized algorithm that solves EXPLORATION with explicit termination with probability at least $1 - \frac{1}{n}$ where n is the size of the ring. Therefore this leaves the open question that whether the problem can be solved by a deterministic algorithm by three non-anonymous robots without edge crossing detection capability.

In this chapter, we answer this question affirmatively, in particular we give a deterministic algorithm that solves EXPLORATION in presence of chirality by three non-anonymous robots without edge-crossing detection capability. As basic ingredients of our algorithm, we introduce a problem called MEETING which is crucial in our attempt to solve the problem of EXPLORATION. In the next chapter, we shall use the ideas that we come up with in this chapter to extend our results in non-chiral settings.

The rest of the chapter is organized as follows, in Section 3.1, we describe the model and terminology used in the paper. In Section 3.2, we describe the algorithm. The correctness proofs are presented in Section 3.3.

3.1 Model and Terminology

We consider a dynamic ring of size n. All nodes of the ring are identical. Each node is connected to its two neighbors via distinctly labeled ports. The labeling of the ports may not be globally consistent and thus might not provide an orientation. We consider a discrete temporal model i.e., time progresses in rounds. In each round at most one edge of the ring may be missing. Thus the ring is connected in each round. Such a network is known in the literature as a 1-interval connected ring.

We consider a team of three robots operating in the ring. The robots do not have any knowledge of the size of the ring. Each robot is provided with memory and computational capabilities. An robot can move from one node to a neighbouring node if the edge between them is not missing. Two robots moving in opposite direction on the same edge are not able to detect each other. An robot can only detect an active robot co-located at the same node i.e., if an robot terminates it becomes undetectable by any other robot. Two robots can communicate with each other only when they are present at the same node. Each robot has a unique identifier which is a bit string of constant length $k > 1$, i.e., the length k of the identifier is the same for each robot. For an robot r, its unique identifier will be denoted by $r.ID$. Also $val(r.ID)$ will denote the numerical value of $r.ID$. For example $val(00110) = 6$, $val(10011) = 19$, etc. Hence for any robot r, $val(r.ID) < 2^k$.

Each robot has a consistent private orientation of the ring, i.e., a consistent notion of left or right. If the left and right of all three robots are the same then we say that the robots have chirality. By clockwise and counterclockwise we shall refer to the orientations of the ring in the usual sense. These terms will be used only for the purpose of description and the robots are unaware of any such global orientation if they do not have chirality. For two robots r_1 and r_2 on the ring, $d^{\circlearrowright}(r_1, r_2)$ and $d^{\circlearrowleft}(r_1, r_2)$ denotes respectively the clockwise and counterclockwise distance from r_1 to r_2. In this chapter we assume that the robots have chirality.

We consider a fully synchronous system, i.e., all three robots are active in each round. In each round, the robots perform the following sequence of operations:

Look: If other robots are present at the node, then the robot exchanges messages with them.

Compute: Based on its local observation, memory and received messages, the robot performs some local computations and determines whether to move or not, and if yes, then in which direction.

Move: If the robot has decided to move in the COMPUTE phase, then the robot attempts to move in the corresponding direction. It will be able to move only if the corresponding edge is not missing. An robot can detect if it has failed to move.

During the execution of algorithm, two robots can meet each other in two possible ways: (1) two robots r_1 and r_2 moving in opposite direction come to the same node, or, (2) an robot r_1 comes to a node where there is a stationary robot r_2. In the second case we say that r_1 *catches* r_2. If two robots r_1, r_2 are moving in opposite direction on the same edge in the same round, then we say that r_1 and r_2 *swaps over an edge*.

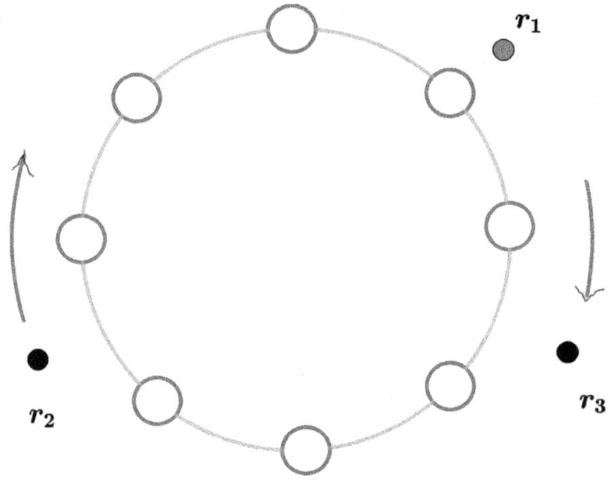

Figure 3.1: The robot with the smallest ID, in this case r_1 stops moving first, during the MEETING protocol

3.2 Description of the Algorithm

Since the robots have agreement in direction we shall use the terms clockwise and counterclockwise instead of right and left respectively. In Section 3.2.0.1, we present an algorithm for MEETING where at least two robots are required to meet at a node. Then in Section 3.2.0.2 we shall use this algorithm as a subroutine to solve EXPLORATION.

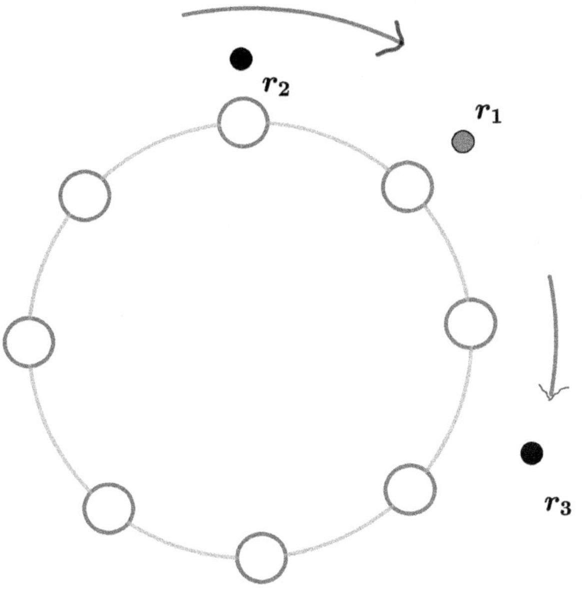

Figure 3.2: If the other two robots keep moving long enough one of them is guaranteed to meet r_1

3.2.0.1 Meeting by robots with Chirality

We have three robots placed arbitrarily at distinct nodes of the ring. Our objective is that at least two of the robots should meet. The algorithm works in several phases. The lengths of the phases are 2^{j+k}, $j = 0, 1, 2, \ldots$. In phase j, an robot r tries to move clockwise for the first $val(r.ID)2^j$ rounds, and then remains stationary for $(2^k - val(r.ID))2^j$ rounds.

Notice that in each phase, the robot with the smallest ID value stops trying to move first, refer to Figure 3.1. The main idea behind the algorithm is that if the remaining robots keep trying to move for long enough, then a meeting should take place. The intuition is the following. Once the first robot stops moving, the remaining two robots are trying to move towards it. If the closer one is not blocked by edge removals in too many rounds then it will be able to catch the

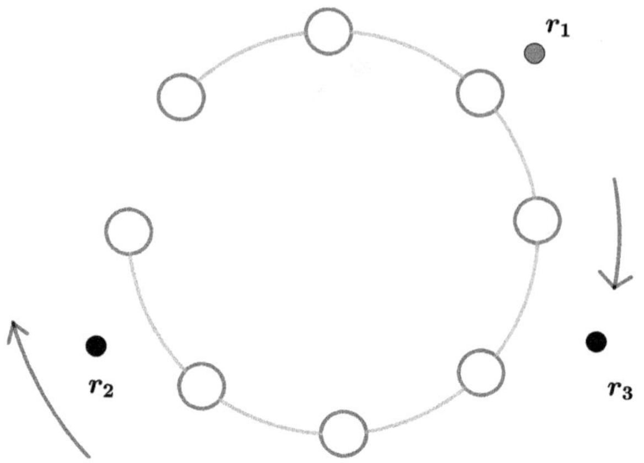

Figure 3.3: The robot r_2 might get stuck due to disappearence of an edge

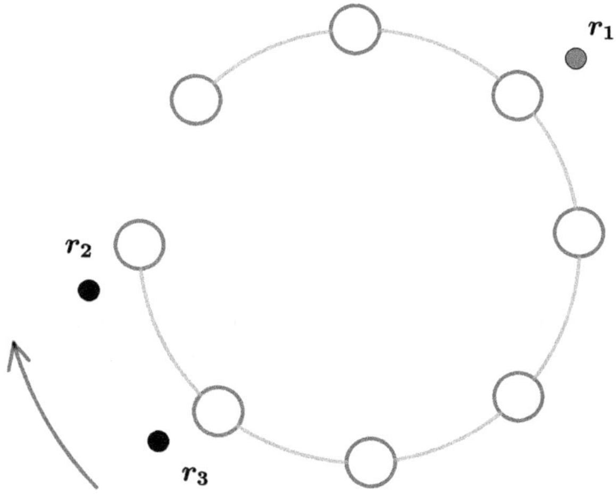

Figure 3.4: In that case r_3 catches up with r_2

static robot within a certain time, refer to Figure 3.2. Otherwise if the robot is blocked for too long, refer to Figure 3.3 then it will get caught by the third robot, refer to Figure 3.4. This is because in the rounds where the robot is blocked, the third robot is able to make progress as at most one edge may disappear in each round. Using this observation, we can show that our algorithm guarantees a meeting at or before the pth phase where $p = \lceil \log 2n \rceil$. So the algorithm solves the problem within $2^k \sum_{i=0}^{p} 2^i < 2^{k+\lceil \log n \rceil+2}$ rounds. This is formally stated in Theorem 3.1. The proof of the theorem is given in Section 3.3.1.

3.2.0.2 Exploration with Termination by robots with Chirality

We consider three robots in the ring having chirality. For simplicity, assume that the robots are initially placed at distinct nodes of the ring. We shall later remove this assumption. Our plan is to first bring two of the robots at the same node using the MEETING algorithm described in Section 3.2.0.1. Then one of them will settle at that node and play the role of landmark node. Then the situation reduces to a setting similar to [71]. However, we cannot use the same algorithm from [71] in our case. This is because unlike in [71] we have to ensure that the robot acting as landmark also terminates. However, our algorithm uses ideas from [71]. We shall now give a description of the algorithm.

Initially all the robots start with their *state* variable set to `search`. Until an robot meets another robot, it executes the MEETING algorithm described in Section 3.2.0.1. Now according to Theorem 3.1, two robots are guaranteed to meet within $2^{k+\lceil \log 2n \rceil+2}$ rounds from the start of the algorithm. On meeting, the robots compare their IDs and the one with smaller ID changes its *state* to `settled` and stops moving. The other robot changes its *winner* variable to *True* and henceforth, abandons its phase-wise movement and attempts to move clockwise in each round. Let us now describe the case when an robot with *state* `search` meets the `settled` robot. If an robot with $winner = False$ encounters the `settled` robot it also abandons its phase-wise movement and henceforth, tries to move in the clockwise direction in every round. If an robot with $winner = True$ meets the `settled` robot r, then it indicates that it is meeting the `settled` robot for the second time and hence all nodes of the ring have been explored. The robot can also calculate the size of the ring as it is equal to the number of successful moves between the two meetings. The robot assigns this value to the variable $RSize$ and also informs the `settled` robot about it. Then the robot will continue to move in the clockwise direction for $2n$ more rounds. Both these robots will terminate after the completion of these $2n$ rounds. Now consider the case when an robot with $state$ = `search` and $winner = True$ meets an robot with $state$ = `search` and $winner = False$. If the robot with $winner = True$ already knows n, i.e., it has visited the `settled` robot twice, then both of them terminates immediately. If the robot with $winner = True$ does not already know n, then it changes its $state$ to `forward` and continues to move in the clockwise direction every round. On the other hand, the robot with $winner = False$ changes its $state$ to `bounce` and starts moving in the counterclockwise direction. This phenomenon is called the formation of `settled-forward-bounce` triplet. In this case, both the robots initiate a variable $TTime$ to keep track of the number of rounds elapsed after triplet formation.

After the triplet is created, the robot with $state$ `forward` will continue to move in clockwise direction. The robot with $state$ `bounce` will move counterclockwise and then on fulfillment of certain conditions, it may change its $state$ to `return` and start moving clockwise. Then it may again change its $state$ to `bounce` and start moving counterclockwise. The period between any two such $state$ changes will be called a *run*. While moving in the clockwise direction with $state$ `forward`, the robot keeps count of the number of successful steps with state `forward` in the variable $FSteps$. The variable $BSteps$ (resp. $RSteps$) is used to keep count of the number of successful steps with state `bounce` (resp. `return`) in the current run. Also while moving in the counterclockwise direction with $state$ `bounce`, the variable $BBlocked$ counts the number of unsuccessful attempts to move in that run. An robot r with $state$ `bounce` will change its $state$ to `return` if one of the following takes place: 1) $r.BBlocked$ exceeds $r.BSteps$ or 2) the robot r encounters the `settled` robot twice in the same run. An robot r with $state$ `return` will change its $state$ to `bounce` if r meets with the robot with $state$ `forward` and $r.RSteps > 2r.BSteps$, where $BSteps$ was counted in the last run with $state$ `bounce`. Here the main idea is that the robots will try to gauge the size of the ring. An robot may be able to find the size n exactly or calculate an upper bound of n. An robot can exactly find n only if it visits the static `settled` robot twice in the same direction. In this case it will also inform the `settled` robot about n. Clearly when this happens the ring has been explored completely. However, the two robots cannot terminate immediately because the third robot is not aware of this. So the robots will remain active till $TTime = 16n$, i.e., $16n$ rounds from the time when the triplet was created. It should be noted here that the `settled` robot initially did not know the time when the triplet was created. It came to know about this from the $TTime$ value of some robot that it met and initiated its own $TTime$ counter accordingly. Now it can be shown that within these $16n$ rounds the third robot will meet one of the two robots that already know n. These two robots will terminate immediately upon meeting. Now consider the case where an robot is able to find an upper bound of n. This happens when one of the following three takes place: 1) the `forward` robot meets the robot with *state* `bounce`, 2) the `forward` robot catches the robot with *state* `return`, 3) the robot with *state* `return` catches the `forward` robot with $RSteps \leq 2BSteps$. It can be shown in each of the cases, these two robots will be able to correctly calculate an upper bound $SBound$ of n. Furthermore these cases imply that the ring has been already explored completely. However, the two robots cannot terminate immediately because the `settled` robot is not aware of this. Therefore in order to acknowledge the `settled` robot, these two robots will start moving in opposite directions for $SBound$ more rounds and then terminate. Clearly one of them will be able to meet the `settled` robot.

The pseudocodes of the described procedure are given in Algorithm 6, 7, 8, 9 and 10. It can be shown that this strategy solves EXPLORATION with explicit termination in $2^{k+\lceil \log n \rceil+3} + 23n = O(n)$ rounds.

This is stated in Theorem 3.2, the supporting lemmas of the theorem proved in Section 3.3.2 and the main theorem is proved in Section 3.3.3.

Algorithm 6: The algorithm executed by an robot r with state `search`

1. Until another robot is found, execute the algorithm for MEETING described in Section 3.2.0.1.

2. Upon the first meeting do the following.

2.1 If two robots are encountered in the first meeting, then set $r.state \leftarrow$ `bounce` and move counterclockwise. Also initiate the counter $r.TTime$. Otherwise if there is exactly one robot r' then do the following.

2.2. If $r'.state =$ `search` and $r'.winner = False$ then do the following. If $val(r.ID) < val(r'.ID)$, then set $r.state \leftarrow$ `settled` and remain at the current node. Otherwise if $val(r.ID) > val(r'.ID)$, then set $r.winner \leftarrow True$ and keep moving clockwise until the next meeting. Also initiate a counter $SCount$ to count the number of successful steps since the first meeting with r'.

2.3. If $r'.state =$ `search` and $r'.winner = True$, then set $r.state \leftarrow$ `bounce` and move counterclockwise. Also initiate the counter $r.TTime$.

2.4. If $r'.state =$ `settled`, then keep moving clockwise until the next meeting.

3. Upon any subsequent meeting do the following.

3.1. If only one robot r' is encountered with $r'.state =$ `search`, then do the following.

3.1.1. If $r'.winner = False$ and $r.RSize = \emptyset$, then set $r.state \leftarrow$ `forward` and move clockwise. Also initiate the counter $r.TTime$.

3.1.2. If $r'.winner = True$ and $r'.RSize = \emptyset$, then set $r.state \leftarrow$ `bounce` and move counterclockwise. Also initiate the counter $r.TTime$. Otherwise, if $r'.winner = True$ and $r'.RSize \neq \emptyset$, then terminate.

3.2. If only one robot r' is encountered with $r'.state =$ `settled`, then do the following.

3.2.1. If $r.winner = True$, then set $r.RSize \leftarrow r.SCount = n$ (since r' is encountered for the second time) and inform r' about n. Keep moving clockwise for $2n$ more rounds and then terminate.

3.2.2. If $r.winner = False$ and $r'.RSize \neq \emptyset$, then terminate.

3.3 If two robots are encountered then there must be an robot r' with $state$ `search`. Then execute **3.1.1.** or **3.1.2.** whichever is applicable.

Algorithm 7: The algorithm executed by an robot r with state `settled`

1. Do not move. Terminate on one of the following conditions.

- **1.1.** If the other two robots are present at the same time and one of them has *state* `forward`, then terminate immediately.
- **1.2.** If an robot r' is encountered such that $r'.SBound \neq \emptyset$, then terminate immediately.
- **1.3.** If n is already known, i.e., $r.RSize \neq \emptyset$, and an robot r' is encountered that does not know n, i.e., $r'.RSize = \emptyset$, then terminate immediately.
- **1.4.** If an robot r' with state `search` informs $r'.RSize = n$, then terminate after $2n$ more rounds.
- **1.5.** If an robot r' with state `forward` or `return` informs $r'.RSize = n$ and $r'.TTime$, then initiate counter $r.TTime$ with starting value $r.TTime \leftarrow r'.TTime$ and terminate after the round when $r.TTime = 16n$.

3.3 Correctness Proofs

3.3.1 Proof of Theorem 3.1

Lemma 3.1. *Let r_1, r_2 and r_3 be three robots in the ring such that at round t, $0 \leq d^{\circlearrowright}(r_1, r_3) < d^{\circlearrowright}(r_1, r_2)$. If r_1 remains static and both r_2 and r_3 try to move clockwise for the next $2n$ rounds, then within these $2n$ rounds either r_2 meets r_1 or r_3 meets r_2.*

Proof. Assume that at round t, $d^{\circlearrowright}(r_1, r_2) = x$ and $d^{\circlearrowright}(r_2, r_3) = y$. We have $x + y \leq n$. Within the next $2n$ rounds, if r_2 is able to move clockwise for at least x rounds, then it will meet r_1 and we are done. So assume that r_2 does not meet r_1. Suppose that r_2 succeeds to make a move $x' < x$ times in the next $2n$ rounds. This means that r_2 remains static for $2n - x'$ rounds. Therefore, r_3 moves clockwise in those $2n - x'$ rounds when r_2 is static. Hence, $d^{\circlearrowright}(r_2, r_3)$ decreases in these rounds. Recall that initially we had $d^{\circlearrowright}(r_2, r_3) = y$. Also, in the x' rounds when r_2 was able to move, $d^{\circlearrowright}(r_2, r_3)$ may or may not have increased depending

Algorithm 8: The algorithm executed by an robot r with state `forward`

1. Until a new meeting, keep moving clockwise. Maintain the counters $r.FSteps \leftarrow$ number of successful steps with state `forward` and $r.TTime \leftarrow$ number of rounds since the triple was formed.

2. If all three robots meet at a node then terminate immediately. Otherwise upon meeting an robot r', do the following.

2.1. If $r.RSize = \emptyset \wedge r'.RSize \neq \emptyset$ or $r.RSize \neq \emptyset \wedge r'.RSize = \emptyset$ then terminate immediately. Otherwise, do the following.

2.2. If $r'.state =$ `settled`, then infer $r.RSize \leftarrow r.SCount = n$ (since r' is encountered for the second time) and inform r' about n. Keep moving clockwise and terminate after the round when $r.TTime = 16n$.

2.3. If $r'.state =$ `bounce`, set $r.SBound \leftarrow r.FSteps + r'.BSteps$. Then keep moving clockwise for $r.SBound$ rounds and then terminate. If the `settled` robot is met meanwhile, then terminate immediately.

2.4. If $r'.state =$ `return`, then do the following.

2.4.1. If r catches r', then set $r.SBound \leftarrow r.FSteps + r'.BSteps$. Then keep moving clockwise for $r.SBound$ rounds and then terminate. If the `settled` robot is met meanwhile, then terminate immediately.

2.4.2. If r' catches r and $r'.Rsteps > 2r'.Bsteps$, then keep moving clockwise until the next meeting. Otherwise if $r'.Rsteps \leq 2r'.Bsteps$, then set $r.SBound \leftarrow r.FSteps + r'.BSteps + 1$. Then keep moving clockwise for $r.SBound$ rounds and then terminate. If the `settled` robot is met meanwhile, then terminate immediately.

Algorithm 9: The algorithm executed by an robot r with state `bounce`

1. Maintain the counters $r.BSteps \leftarrow$ number of successful steps with state `bounce` in the current run, $r.BBlocked \leftarrow$ number of unsuccessful attempts with state `bounce` in the current run and $r.TTime \leftarrow$ number of rounds since the triple was formed. Until a new meeting or fulfillment of the condition $r.BBlocked > r.BSteps$, keep moving in the counterclockwise direction. If $r.BBlocked > r.BSteps$ is satisfied, change $r.state \leftarrow$ **`return`** and move clockwise.

2. If all three robots meet at a node then terminate immediately. Otherwise upon meeting any robot r', do the following.

   2.1. If $r.RSize = \emptyset \wedge r'.RSize \neq \emptyset$ or $r.RSize \neq \emptyset \wedge r'.RSize = \emptyset$ then terminate immediately. Otherwise, do the following.

   2.2. If $r'.state =$ **`settled`** then do the following.

   2.2.1. If it is the first meeting with r' in the same run, then keep moving counterclockwise until a new meeting or fulfillment of the condition $r.BBlocked > r.BSteps$. Also initiate a counter $SCount$ to count the number of successful steps since the first meeting with r' in the current run.

   2.2.2. If it is the second meeting with r' in the same run, then set $r.RSize \leftarrow r.SCount = n$. Change $r.state \leftarrow$ **`return`** and move clockwise.

   2.3. If $r'.state =$ **`forward`**, then set $r.SBound \leftarrow r'.FSteps + r.BSteps$. Then keep moving counterclockwise for $r.SBound$ rounds and then terminate. If the **`settled`** robot is met meanwhile, then terminate immediately.

Algorithm 10: The algorithm executed by an robot r with state `return`

1. If the size of the ring is already known, i.e., $r.RSize = n$, then keep moving clockwise and terminate after the round when $r.TTime = 16n$. Otherwise, keep moving in the clockwise direction until a new meeting. Maintain the counters $r.RSteps \leftarrow$ number of successful steps with state `return` in the current run and $r.TTime \leftarrow$ number of rounds since the triple was formed.

2. If all three robots meet at a node then terminate immediately. Otherwise upon meeting any robot r', do the following.

2.1. If $r.RSize = \emptyset \wedge r'.RSize \neq \emptyset$ or $r.RSize \neq \emptyset \wedge r'.RSize = \emptyset$ then terminate immediately. Otherwise, do the following.

2.2. If $r'.state =$ `forward`, then do the following.

2.2.1. If r' catches r, then set $r.SBound \leftarrow r.FSteps + r'.BSteps$. Then move counterclockwise for $r.SBound$ rounds and then terminate. If the `settled` robot is met meanwhile, then terminate immediately.

2.2.2. If r catches r' then do the following.

2.2.2.1. If $r.RSteps \leq 2r.BSteps$ then set $r.SBound \leftarrow r.FSteps + r'.BSteps + 1$. Then move counterclockwise for $r.SBound$ rounds and then terminate. If the `settled` robot is met meanwhile, then terminate immediately.

2.2.2.2. Otherwise, if $r.RSteps > 2r.BSteps$, then change $r.state \leftarrow$ `bounce` and move counterclockwise.

on whether r_3 respectively failed or succeeded to move in those rounds. Now notice that

$$\begin{aligned} 2n - x' &\geq n + x + y - x' && \text{(since } n \geq x + y\text{)} \\ &> n + y && \text{(since } x > x'\text{)} \\ &> x' + y && \text{(since } n > x'\text{)} \end{aligned}$$

This implies that r_3 will catch r_2. This completes the proof that within the $2n$ rounds either r_2 meets r_1 or r_3 meets r_2. □

Using Lemma 3.1, we shall prove Theorem 3.1 which states that our algorithm ensures a meeting within $2^{k+\lceil \log n \rceil+2}$ rounds.

Theorem 3.1. *The above algorithm solves* MEETING *for three robots with chirality. The algorithm ensures that the meeting takes place within* $2^{k+\lceil \log n \rceil+2}$ *rounds.*

Proof. Let $p = \lceil \log 2n \rceil = \lceil \log n \rceil + 1$. Hence p is the smallest positive integer such that $2^p \geq 2n$. If two robots have met before the pth phase, then we are done. If not, we show that a pair of robots is guaranteed to meet during the pth phase. Recall that in this phase, an robot r should (attempt to) rotate clockwise for $val(r.ID)2^p$ rounds, and then remain stationary for the remaining $(2^k - val(r.ID))2^p$ rounds. Let r_1 be the first robot to come to rest in that phase, say at round t. Let r_2 be the robot closest to r_1 in the counterclockwise direction and r_3 be the third robot. We have $val(r_2.ID)2^p - val(r_1.ID)2^p \geq 2n$ and $val(r_3.ID)2^p - val(r_1.ID)2^p \geq 2n$. This implies that both r_2 and r_3 attempts to move for at least $2n$ rounds after r_1 comes to rest at round t. By Lemma 3.1, either r_2 and r_1 meets, or r_3 and r_2 meets. So the meeting takes place within $2^k \sum_{i=0}^{p} 2^i < 2^{k+\lceil \log n \rceil+2}$ rounds. □

3.3.2 Correctness Proof of Lemmas prerequisite to Theorem 3.2

Lemma 3.2. *There exists a round* $T_1 \leq 2^{k+\lceil \log n \rceil+2}$ *when two of the robots with state* **`search`** *meet and a* **`settled`** *robot is created.*

Proof. This follows from Theorem 3.1 since the robots execute the algorithm from Section 3.2.0.1 until they meet another robot. □

Lemma 3.3. *Suppose that r_1 and r_2 meets at round T_1 and r_1 becomes* `settled`*. There is a round T_2, with $T_1 < T_2 < 2^{k+\lceil \log n \rceil+3}$, when the third robot r_3 meets either r_1 or r_2.*

Proof. At round T_1, r_1 and r_2 meet and r_1 becomes `settled`. After T_1, r_2 is trying to move clockwise in each round. On the other hand, since r_3 is still executing the MEETING algorithm, it will try to move clockwise on some rounds and on other rounds, will not try to move at all. Now if both r_2 and r_3 try to move clockwise for some $2n$ consecutive rounds together, then by Lemma 3.1 either r_2 meets r_3 or r_3 meets r_1. Clearly, this is guaranteed to happen in any phase l, where $l \geq p = \lceil \log 2n \rceil$. Now suppose that T_1 belongs to the jth phase. By Lemma 3.2, $j \leq p$. If $j < p$, then the required meeting should take place in or before the pth phase and if $j = p$, then the required meeting will take place in pth or $(p+1)$th phase. Therefore, we have $T_2 \leq \sum_{i=0}^{p+1} 2^{i+k} < 2^{k+\lceil \log n \rceil+3}$. □

Lemma 3.4. *Within T_2+$4n$ rounds either all three robots terminate or a* `settled-forward-bounce` *triple is created.*

Proof. Recall that by Lemma 3.3, at round T_2, either r_3 meets r_1 or r_3 meets r_2. In the latter case, a `settled-forward-bounce` triple is created and we are done. So consider the other case where r_3 meets the `settled` robot r_1. Before this meeting, r_3 was trying to move clockwise in some rounds, while in other rounds, it was not trying to move at all. After meeting r_1, r_3 will try moving clockwise in each round. Then by Lemma 3.1 within $2n$ rounds (i.e., within $T_2 + 2n$ rounds from the beginning), either r_2 meets r_1 again, or r_3 meets r_2. In the latter case, a `settled-forward-bounce` triple is created, and we are done. So consider the other case where r_2 meets r_1 for the second time. Thus r_2 finds out n (the size of the ring) and also informs r_1 about it. Then r_2 will keep moving clockwise for $2n$ more rounds and then terminate. Also r_1 will remain active for $2n$ more rounds and then terminate. Now within these $2n$ rounds, r_3 will meet either r_1 or r_2 and terminate immediately. Therefore, within $T_2 + 4n$ rounds either all three robots terminate or a `settled-forward-bounce` triple is created. □

Suppose that at round $T_3 \leq T_2 + 4n$ a `settled-forward-bounce` triple is formed. We shall denote by r_1, r_2 and r_3 the robots with states `settled`, `forward` and `bounce` respectively. We shall say that the robots r_2 and r_3 *agree on an upper bound of* n if one of the following events occur at any round after T_3. We show in Lemma 3.5 that indeed if one of the following events take place then the robots can find an upper bound of n.

Event 1. The robot r_2 with state `forward` and r_3 with state `bounce` meet each other at a node and neither of them know n.

Event 2. The robot r_2 with state `forward` catches r_3 with state `return` at a node and neither of them know n.

Event 3. The robot r_3 with state `return` catches r_2 with state `forward` at a node and $r_3.Rsteps \leq 2r_3.Bsteps$ and neither of them know n.

Lemma 3.5. *If one of Event 1-3 takes place, then*

1. *exploration is complete,*
2. *r_2 and r_3 can infer an upper bound N of n such that $n \leq N \leq 3n$ and will set it as $SBound$.*

Proof. **Event 1.** Consider a run of r_3, starting when it met r_2 and changed its state to `bounce` and ending when it met r_2 again (Event 1). Then it is easy to see that all nodes of the ring have been explored by r_2 and r_3. Upon meeting, both r_2 and r_3 set $SBound = r_2.FSteps + r_3.BSteps$. Clearly $SBound \geq n$. Also since both r_2 and r_3 do not know n, $r_2.FSteps < n$ and $r_3.BSteps < 2n$. To see the first inequality observe that if $r_2.FSteps \geq n$ then it implies that r_2 with *state* `forward` has met r_1. But recall that r_2 has already met r_1 before when it was in *state* `search` and moving in the same direction. This implies that r_2 can infer n by counting the number of successful steps since the first meeting. For the second inequality observe that if $r_3.BSteps \geq 2n$ then it implies r_3 has met r_1 twice in the same run and therefore can infer n by counting the number of successful steps from the first and second meeting. Hence $SBound < 3n$.

Event 2. Suppose that at some node u, r_2 and r_3 meet each other and continue moving in clockwise (with state `forward`) and counterclockwise (with state `bounce`) direction respectively. Then suppose that at node v, r_3 changes its state to `return` and its direction to clockwise. Then after sometime r_2 catches r_3 (Event 2). Clearly all nodes in the counterclockwise path from u to v have been visited by r_3 and all nodes in the clockwise path from u to v have been visited by r_2. Hence all nodes in the ring have been together explored by r_2 and r_3. Upon meeting, they both set $SBound = r_2.FSteps + r_3.BSteps$. Clearly $r_3.BSteps = d^{\circlearrowleft}(u, v)$ and $r_2.FStep \geq d^{\circlearrowright}(u, v)$. Hence $SBound \geq d^{\circlearrowleft}(u, v) + d^{\circlearrowright}(u, v) = n$. Also by previous argument $SBound < 3n$.

Event 3. Suppose that at some time r_2 and r_3 meet each other at node u and continue moving in clockwise (with state `forward`) and counterclockwise (with state `bounce`) direction respectively. Then at some time r_3 changes its state to `return` (when we have $r_3.BBlocked = r_3.BSteps + 1$) and its direction to clockwise. Then after sometime it catches r_2 and finds that $r_3.RSteps \leq 2r_3.BSteps$ (Event 3). We show that this implies that exploration is complete. If r_2 and r_3 swapped over an edge at some round in between, then it implies that all nodes of the ring have been explored and we are done. Otherwise we have $r_3.RSteps = r_3.BSteps + r_2.FSteps$ at the time of meeting. Since $r_3.RSteps \leq 2r_3.BSteps$, we have $r_2.FSteps \leq r_3.BSteps$. Also recall that $r_3.BBlocked = r_3.BSteps + 1$. Now if r_2 had been able to successfully execute a move during each of those rounds when r_3 was blocked with state `bounce`, we must have had $r_2.FSteps > r_3.BSteps$. But since $r_2.FSteps \leq r_3.BSteps$, r_2 with state `forward` and r_3 with state `bounce` must have been blocked at the same round. This can only happen if r_2 and r_3 are blocked on two ends of the same missing edge. This implies that the ring has been explored. Upon meeting both r_2 and r_3 set $SBound = r_2.FSteps + r_3.BSteps + 1$. If they had swapped over an edge then clearly $SBound \geq n$. Otherwise we showed that r_2 and r_3 were blocked at two adjacent nodes of the ring, say v and w respectively. Then $r_3.BSteps \geq d^{\circlearrowleft}(u, w)$ and $r_2.FStep \geq d^{\circlearrowright}(u, v)$. Hence $SBound \geq d^{\circlearrowright}(u, v) + d^{\circlearrowleft}(u, w) + 1 = n$. Also by previous argument $SBound < 3n + 1 \implies SBound \leq 3n$.

□

Lemma 3.6. *Suppose that r_2 and r_3 meet at some round T and r_3 changes its state to* `bounce`. *If they do not meet again for $10n$ rounds then all three robots are guaranteed to find out n*

Proof. Assume that r_2 and r_3 do not meet for $10n$ rounds from T. Now at round T, r_3 changes its state to `bounce`. By round $T+4n$ either r_3 has made $2n$ successful moves in the counterclockwise direction or the condition $BBlocked > BSteps$ is fulfilled. In the former case r_3 finds out n and changes its state to `return`. In the latter case also r_3 changes its state to `return`. Therefore within $4n$ rounds r_3 is guaranteed to start moving in clockwise direction, say at round $T' \leq T + 4n$ i.e., from T' onwards both r_2 and r_3 are moving in the same direction. Therefore within $2n$ rounds either r_2 and r_3 meet each other or one of them meets r_1. Since we assumed that r_2 and r_3 do not meet, the latter takes place.

Case 1: Suppose that r_1 meets r_2. Then both r_1 and r_2 find out n (if not already known). Within $2n$ rounds r_3 comes to r_1 and also find out n (if not already known). So within $4n$ rounds from T', i.e. $8n$ rounds from T all three robots find out n.

Case 2: Suppose that r_1 meets r_3. Then within next $2n$ rounds r_2 meets r_1. Then by the arguments of Case 1, all three robots will find out n within next $2n$ rounds. Therefore, within $6n$ rounds from T', i.e., $10n$ rounds from T, all three robots find out n. □

Lemma 3.7. *Within $16n$ rounds after T_3, either all three robots find out n or r_2, r_3 agree on an upper bound of n.*

Proof. Let us refer to the meeting of r_2 and r_3 at round T_3 as their 1st meeting. If r_2 and r_3 do not meet each other again for $16n$ rounds, then by Lemma 3.6 all three robots will find out n, and we are done. Therefore we assume that r_2 and r_3 meet again at least once after T_3 within $16n$ rounds. Let t_i denote the time between the ith and $(i+1)$th meeting. In view of Lemma 3.6 we can assume that $t_i \leq 10n$ because otherwise all three robots will find out n, and we are done. Also if any one of these meetings is of the type Event 1-3, then we are done as such meetings allow r_2 and r_3 to agree on an upper bound of n (c.f. Lemma 3.5). So let us assume that such meetings do not occur. Therefore in each meeting after T_3, r_3 with state `return` catches r_2 with state `forward`. If at the time of any meeting after T_3, r_3 is aware of n (by meeting r_1 twice in a run with *state* `bounce`), then we are done. This is because r_2 finds out n from r_3 at the time of the meeting and r_1 also had already found out n from r_3. So assume that this does not happen at any of the meetings. Notice that if we can show that one such meeting takes place after r_2 visits r_1, then we are done. To see this observe that if r_2 visits r_1 then r_2 finds out n and also informs r_1 about it. Then r_3 also comes to know about n in the next meeting between r_2 and r_3. So we complete the proof by showing that a meeting between r_2 and r_3 takes place within $16n$ rounds from T_3 with r_2 having already met r_1.

Recall that t_i denotes the time between the ith and $(i+1)$th meeting. Let fs_i, bs_i and rs_i denote the number of successful steps made during this time by r_2 with state `forward`, r_3 with state `bounce` and r_3 with state `return` respectively. First we claim that if r_2 and r_3 swap over an edge between their ith and $(i+1)$th meeting, then r_2 will find out n before the $(i+1)$th meeting. Since the $(i+1)$th meeting is not of the type Event 3, we have $rs_i > 2bs_i$. If $bs_i > n$, then $rs_i > 2n > n$. This means that r_3 with state `return` meet r_1. But then r_2 must have met r_1 before this meeting and found out n. So let $bs_i \leq n$. Then it is not difficult to see that $bs_i + fs_i = n + rs_i$. Again using $rs_i > 2bs_i$, we have $fs_i > n + bs_i > n$. This implies that r_2 have met r_1 and found out n. So assume that r_2 and r_3 do not swap in between the ith and $(i+1)$th meeting. Then we have $rs_i = bs_i + fs_i$. Furthermore we have $t_i \leq 2bs_i + 1 + fs_i + rs_i$. Here $2bs_i + 1$ is an upper bound on the time needed by r_3 to switch state from `bounce` to `return`. To see this, recall that r_3 changes its state to `return` if one of the following takes place: (1) it finds out n by meeting r_1 twice, (2) $r_3.BBlocked > r_3.BSteps$ is satisfied. Since we assumed that (1) does not take place, r_3 must have changed its state to `return` because of (2). Since this happens when the number of failed attempts to move exceeds the number of successful moves, we can conclude that $2bs_i+1$ is an upper bound on the time needed by r_3 to switch state from `bounce` to `return`. Also, fs_i+rs_i is an upper bound on the time needed for r_3 with state `return` to catch r_2. This is because the number of successful moves by r_3 is rs_i and the number of failed attempts to move by r_3 is bounded by fs_i since each failed move by r_3 implies a successful move by r_2. Substituting the value of rs_i in the inequality we get, $t_i \leq 3bs_i + 2fs_i + 1$. Since this meeting is not of the type Event 3, we have $rs_i > 2bs_i \implies fs_i > bs_i$. Therefore $t_i < 6fs_i$. Let k be the smallest integer such that $t_1+\ldots+t_k \geq 6n$. So we have $6n \leq t_1+t_2+\ldots+t_k < 6(fs_1+fs_2+\ldots fs_k)$ $\implies n < fs_1+fs_2+\ldots fs_k$. This implies that r_2 makes enough progress to meet r_1 before the $(k+1)$th meeting. Therefore after the $(k+1)$th meeting all three robots have found out n. It remains to show that this meeting takes place within $16n$ rounds from T_3. For this observe the following. It follows from the definition of k (which implies that $t_1 + \ldots + t_{k-1} < 6n$) and the fact that $t_k \leq 10n$ that $t_1 + \ldots + t_k < 16n$.

□

Lemma 3.8. *Within $19n$ rounds after T_3 exploration of the ring is complete and all three robots terminate.*

Proof. By Lemma 3.7 within $16n$ rounds after T_3 either all three robots find out n or r_2, r_3 agree on an upper bound of n. In the former case the robots will terminate when $TTime = 16n$, i.e., after $16n$ rounds from T_3. Now in the latter case when r_2 and r_3 meet at a node to agree on an upper bound N of n, they will move in opposite directions for N more rounds. Within these N rounds one of them will meet r_1 and both will terminate. The other robots will terminate after the completion of these N rounds. Recall that by Lemma 3.5, $N < 3n$. Hence in this case all the three robots terminate within $19n$ rounds after T_3.

□

3.3.3 The Main Result

From the discussions and the results proved in the above subsection we can finally arrive at the following conclusion,

Theorem 3.2. EXPLORATION *with explicit termination is solvable by three robots with chirality in* $2^{k+\lceil \log n \rceil+3} + 23n = O(n)$ *rounds.*

Proof. By Lemma 3.8, the exploration is complete and all three robots terminate within $T_3 + 19n$ rounds. By Lemma 3.4, $T_3 \leq T_2 + 4n$ and by Lemma 3.3, $T_2 < 2^{k+\lceil \log n \rceil+3}$. Therefore our algorithm solves EXPLORATION with explicit termination by three robots with chirality in $2^{k+\lceil \log n \rceil+3} + 23n = O(2^k n)$ rounds.

□

Recall that we assumed that the robots are placed initially at distinct nodes of the ring. We now show that this assumption is not necessary if the initial configuration has two robots r_1, r_2 at the same node and the third robot r_3 at a different node. Then the case reduces to the situation when the first meeting takes place. Then r_1 and r_2 will change their *state* to `settled` and `forward` while r_3 will execute the MEETING algorithm with *state* `search`. The algorithm will progress as before and achieve exploration with termination.

If all three robots are in the same node in the initial configuration then the three robots will compare their identifiers and will change their *state* to `settled`, `forward` and `bounce` accordingly. Again, the algorithm will progress as before and achieve exploration with termination.

3.4 Concluding Remarks

In this chapter we have solved the problem of EXPLORATION with only three robots, without landmark. Here we have assumed chirality, i.e., the robots have a common clockwise and anti-clockwise direction. In the next chapter, we shall solve the problem by removing the assumption of chirality.

Chapter 4

Exploration of a Dynamic Ring without Landmark in the absence of Chirality

In Chapter 3, we solved the EXPLORATION problem in a dynamic ring without landmark but in the presence of chirality. In this chapter, we will solve the problem in the absence of chirality. The techniques we developed in the previous chapter is very crucial as we shall employ the same techniques with some minor operational changes. First of all we shall see what are the challenges possessed in solving this problem due to the absence of chirality. We must note that a crucial part of our algorithm in Chapter 3 is ensuring that two robots must meet at a node. But in the absence of chirality determining the time bound within which two robots are guaranteed to meet is a problem. Note that in Chapter 3 ensuring that two robots meet had been the first step in designing the algorithm for exploration. But in the absence of chirality, the whole idea becomes inapplicable.

Therefore we define and solve a new problem called CONTIGUOUS AGREEMENT which requires the robots to agree on some common direction for some number of consecutive rounds. Then we solve MEETING in the absence of chirality by using these two algorithms as subroutine. In particular, the main idea is to simulate the MEETING algorithm with chirality in the period when the robots agree on a common direction. Our Contiguous Agreement protocol can be useful for solving other problems as it can be used as a tool to transform certain algorithms that functions in presence of chirality to algorithms that work without chirality. After meeting, one of the robots will become landmark as planned. From there we solve Exploration with termination using a strategy which is partly similar to [71]. Overall, the round complexity of our algorithm is $\Theta(n)$, where n is the size of the ring. This is asymptotically optimal as there are n nodes to be explored and in each round, three robots can visit at most three nodes. Furthermore, our algorithm solves the problem with optimum number of robots as in view of the impossibility results of [71], the problem cannot be solved with two robots in this setting.

The chapter is organized as follows. We discuss about the model and basic assumptions in Section 4.1. Then in Section 4.2, we introduce and solve a new problem called Contiguous Agreement. Then in Section 4.3 we use the Contiguous Agreement algorithm to solve Meeting. Finally in Section 4.4 we solve Exploration with explicit termination without chirality.

4.1 Model and Definitions

The model that we describe here is almost same as that of Chapter 3. But still the details are repeated for clarity's sake.

We consider a dynamic ring of size n. All nodes of the ring are identical. Each node is connected to its two neighbors via distinctly labeled ports. The labeling of the ports may not be globally consistent and thus might not provide an orientation. We consider a discrete temporal model i.e., time progresses in rounds. In each round at most one edge of the ring may be missing. Thus the ring is connected in each round. Such a network is known in the literature as a 1-interval connected ring.

We consider a team of three robots operating in the ring. The robots do not have any knowledge of the size of the ring. Each robot is provided with memory and computational capabilities. An robot can move from one node to a neighbouring node if the edge between them is not missing. Two robots moving in opposite direction on the same edge are not able to detect each other. An robot can only detect an active robot co-located at the same node i.e., if an robot terminates it becomes undetectable by any other robot. Two robots can communicate with each other only when they are present at the same node. Each robot has a unique identifier which is a bit string of constant length $k > 1$, i.e., the length k of the identifier is the same for each robot. For an robot r, its unique identifier will be denoted by $r.ID$. Also $val(r.ID)$ will denote the numerical value of $r.ID$. For example $val(00110) = 6$, $val(10011) = 19$, etc. Hence for any robot r, $val(r.ID) < 2^k$.

Each robot has a consistent private orientation of the ring, i.e., a consistent notion of left or right. In this chapter the robots are unaware of any such global orientation i.e., they do not have chirality.

We consider a fully synchronous system, i.e., all three robots are active in each round. In each round, the robots perform the following sequence of operations:

Look: If other robots are present at the node, then the robot exchanges messages with them.

Compute: Based on its local observation, memory and received messages, the robot performs some local computations and determines whether to move or not, and if yes, then in which direction.

Move: If the robot has decided to move in the COMPUTE phase, then the robot attempts to move in the corresponding direction. It will be able to move only if the corresponding edge is not missing. An robot can detect if it has failed to move.

During the execution of algorithm, two robots can meet each other in two possible ways: (1) two robots r_1 and r_2 moving in opposite direction come to the same node, or, (2) an robot r_1 comes to a node where there is a stationary robot r_2. In the second case we say that r_1 *catches* r_2. If two robots r_1, r_2 are moving in opposite direction on the same edge in the same round, then we say that r_1 and r_2 *swaps over an edge.*

4.2 Contiguous Agreement

In this section we define a new problem called Contiguous Agreement. Three robots with unique identifiers are placed at three different nodes in the ring. In each round, each robot chooses a direction according to a deterministic algorithm based on its ID and current round. The requirement of the problem is that the robots have to choose the same direction for some N consecutive rounds where N is a constant unknown to the robots.

Before presenting the algorithm, we describe the construction of modified identifiers which will be used in the algorithm. Recall that $r.ID$ is a binary string of length k. We now describe the construction of the corresponding modified identifier $r.MID$ which is a binary string of length $\frac{k(k-1)}{2}+k+1$. We shall first concatenate a string of length $\frac{k(k-1)}{2}$ at end of $r.ID$. Let us write $\frac{k(k-1)}{2}=l$. To define the string, we shall identify each position of the string as, instead of an integer from $[l]=\{1,\ldots,l\}$, a 2-tuple from the set $S=\{(u,v)\in[k]\times[k]\mid u<v\}$. In order to formally describe this, let us define a bijection $\phi:S\to[l]$ in the following way. Notice that $|S|=l$. Arrange the elements of S in lexicographic order. For any $(u,v)\in S$, we define $\phi((u,v))$ to be the position of (u,v) in this arrangement. For example, if $k=4$, then the elements of S, arranged in lexicographic order, are (1,2), (1,3), (1,4), (2,3), (2,4), (3,4). Therefore, we have $\phi((1,2))=1$, $\phi((1,3))=2$, $\phi((1,4))=3$, $\phi((2,3))=4$, $\phi((2,4))=5$ and $\phi((3,4))=6$. Now we define the string of length l that will be concatenated with $r.ID$. The ith bit of the string is the $\mathbb{Z}_2$ sum of the uth and vth bit of $r.ID$ where $(u,v)=\phi^{-1}(i)$. After the concatenation, we get a string of length $k+l=k+\frac{k(k-1)}{2}$. Finally we append 0 at the beginning of this string to obtain $r.MID$ of length $\frac{k(k-1)}{2}+k+1$ (See Fig. 4.1).

We now present the algorithm that solves Contiguous Agreement. The algorithm works in phases with the length of the phases being $2^j\left(\frac{k(k-1)}{2}+k+1\right)$, $j=$

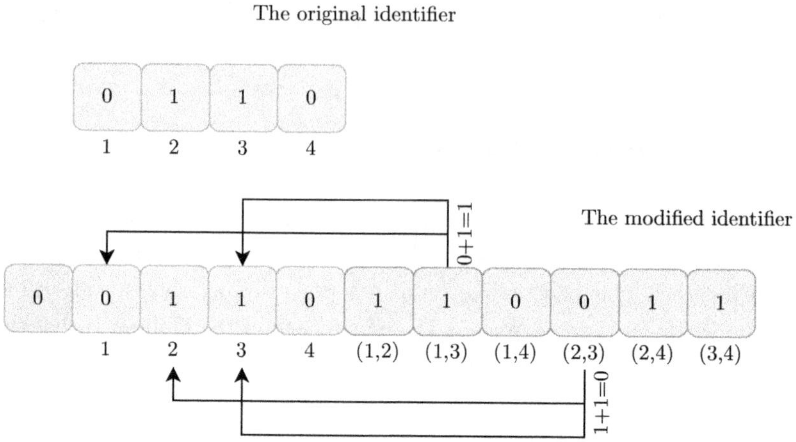

Figure 4.1: The construction of the modified identifier.

$0, 1, 2, \ldots$. For a string S and a positive integer t, let $Dup(S, t)$ denote the string obtained by repeating t times each bit of string S. For example, $Dup(101, 3) =$ 111000111. For the jth phase, the robot r computes $Dup(r.MID, 2^j)$. Notice that the length of the jth phase is equal to the length of $Dup(r.MID, 2^j)$. In the ith round of the jth phase, r moves left if the ith bit of $Dup(r.MID, 2^j)$ is 0 and otherwise moves right.

The idea behind the algorithm is the following. Let us first look at the 0th phase. If the local orientations of all three robots are the same (say left = counterclockwise for each robot) then all three robots will choose the same direction in the first round. This is because MIDs of all robots start with 0 and in the first round all robots choose left which is the counterclockwise direction. Now if the local orientations of all three robots are not the same, still two of the robots will be in agreement. There are three possible cases based on which two robots have the same local orientation. Notice if there is an index where the bit of the MIDs of those two robots are equal, but is different from that of third robot, then all robots will choose the same direction in the round corresponding to that index. It can be shown that such indices exist for each of the three possible cases. This implies that there is a round in the 0th phase in which all three robots choose the same direction. Hence for $j = \lceil \log N \rceil$, the robots will choose the same direction for N consecutive rounds in the jth phase. The formal proof of correctness of algorithm is given below.

Theorem 4.1. *There is an algorithm that solves* CONTIGUOUS AGREEMENT.

Proof. Let us denote the three robots by r_1, r_2 and r_3. For a binary string S and an index $1 \leq \alpha \leq |S|$, we denote by $S[\alpha]$ the αth bit of S. We first show that in the 0th phase, there is a round in which all three robots choose the same direction. In the 0th phase, each robot r_i uses the string $Dup(r_i.MID, 2^0) = r_i.MID$ to set its direction. First consider the case where all three agree on the orientation, say the left according to each of the robots is the counterclockwise direction. Clearly if there is an index α where the strings $r_1.MID$, $r_2.MID$ and $r_3.MID$ have the same bit, i.e., $r_1.MID[\alpha] = r_2.MID[\alpha] = r_3.MID[\alpha]$, then the robots will decide the same the direction in the αth round of the 0th phase. Now suppose that the robots do not agree on orientation. Consider the case where left according to r_1, r_2 is the counterclockwise direction (i.e., r_1 and r_2 have agreement on orientation), while left according to r_3 is the clockwise direction. Clearly in this case, if there is an index α such that $r_1.MID[\alpha] = r_2.MID[\alpha] \neq r_3.MID[\alpha]$, then the robots will decide the same the direction in the αth round of the 0th phase. Therefore, it follows from the above discussion that it suffices to show that $\exists$ indices α, β, γ and η such that,

1. $r_1.MID[\alpha] = r_2.MID[\alpha] = r_3.MID[\alpha]$
2. $r_1.MID[\beta] = r_2.MID[\beta] \neq r_3.MID[\beta]$
3. $r_1.MID[\gamma] = r_3.MID[\gamma] \neq r_2.MID[\gamma]$
4. $r_2.MID[\eta] = r_3.MID[\eta] \neq r_1.MID[\eta]$

Recall that each of the strings start with 0. Hence, we have $\alpha = 1$. Since $r_1.ID \neq r_2.ID$, $\exists$ an index a so that $r_1.ID[a] \neq r_2.ID[a]$. Without loss of generality, let $r_3.ID[a] = r_1.ID[a]$, i.e., $r_1.ID[a] = r_3.ID[a] \neq r_2.ID[a]$. So we let $\gamma = a + 1$

which fulfills the requirement that $r_1.MID[\gamma] = r_3.MID[\gamma] \neq r_2.MID[\gamma]$. We add 1 here because of the 0 appended at the beginning of the MIDs. Similarly since $r_1.ID \neq r_3.ID$, $\exists$ an index $b \neq a$ so that $r_1.ID[b] \neq r_3.ID[b]$. Without loss of generality, let $r_2.ID[b] = r_1.ID[b]$, i.e., $r_1.ID[b] = r_2.ID[b] \neq r_3.ID[b]$. So we let $\beta = b+1$. So now it remains to find the index η. We take η to be the index of MID where we put the sum of the βth bit of MID ($\beta - 1$th bit of ID) and the γth bit of MID (γ − 1th bit of ID). We have to show that $r_2.MID[\eta] = r_3.MID[\eta]$ $\neq r_1.MID[\eta]$. For the equality, observe the following.

$$\begin{aligned}
r_2.MID[\eta] &= r_2.MID[\beta] + r_2.MID[\gamma] \\
&= (1 + r_3.MID[\beta]) + (1 + r_3.MID[\gamma]) \quad (\text{for } x, y \in \mathbb{Z}_2, x \neq y \iff x = y + 1) \\
&= r_3.MID[\beta] + r_3.MID[\gamma] \\
&= r_3.MID[\eta]
\end{aligned}$$

To prove the inequality, we assume for the sake of contradiction that $r_1.MID[\eta] = r_2.MID[\eta]$. This leads to a contradiction as shown in the following.

$$\begin{aligned}
r_1.MID[\eta] &= r_2.MID[\eta] \\
\implies r_1.MID[\beta] + r_1.MID[\gamma] &= r_2.MID[\beta] + r_2.MID[\gamma] \\
\implies r_2.MID[\beta] + (1 + r_2.MID[\gamma]) &= r_2.MID[\beta] + r_2.MID[\gamma] \\
\implies 1 &= 0
\end{aligned}$$

Hence, we show that there is round in the 0th phase where all three robots will decide the same direction. It immediately follows from the proof that there are 2^j consecutive rounds in the jth phase where all three robots will choose the same direction. Hence, for $j = \lceil \log N \rceil$, the robots will choose the same direction for N consecutive rounds in the jth phase.

□

4.3 Meeting by robots without Chirality

In Section 3.2.0.1, we describe an algorithm that solves MEETING by robots with chirality. In the current setting where robots do not have chirality, the main idea is to use the strategy of CONTIGUOUS AGREEMENT so that the robots can implicitly agree on a common direction and solve MEETING by employing the strategy from section 3.2.0.1. Similar to the algorithm for CONTIGUOUS AGREEMENT, our algorithm for MEETING also works in phases. In the algorithm for CONTIGUOUS AGREEMENT the length of the phases were $2^j\left(\frac{k(k-1)}{2}+k+1\right)$, $j=0,1,2,\ldots$. For MEETING, the phases will be of length $2^{j+k}\left(\frac{k(k-1)}{2}+k+1\right)$, $j=0,1,2,\ldots$. In the jth phase of the algorithm an robot r uses the string $Dup(r.MID, 2^{j+k})$ to decide its movement. Notice that the length of $Dup(r.MID, 2^{j+k})$ is equal to the length of the jth phase. The string $Dup(r.MID, 2^{j+k})$ is a concatenation of $\left(\frac{k(k-1)}{2}+k+1\right)$ blocks of length 2^{j+k} where each block consists of all 0's or all 1's. Our plan is to simulate the MEETING algorithm from Section 3.2.0.1. So, in the 2^{j+k} rounds corresponding to each block, the robot r will (try to) move in the first $val(r.ID)2^j$ rounds and will be stationary for the remaining $\left(2^k - val(r.ID)\right)2^j$ rounds. If the block consists of 0's, then the movement will be towards left and otherwise towards right. It can be shown that the algorithm solves the problem within $k^2 2^{k+\lceil\log n\rceil+3}$ rounds as stated in Theorem 4.2. Refer to Figure 4.3.

Theorem 4.2. MEETING *is solvable by three robots without chirality in* $k^2 2^{k+\lceil\log n\rceil+3}$ *rounds.*

Proof. Let $p=\lceil\log 2n\rceil$. If two robots have met before the pth phase, then we are done. Otherwise, we show that a pair of robots must meet during the pth phase. Recall that in the pth phase, an robot r uses the bits of the string $Dup(r.MID, 2^{p+k})$ to decide its movement in each round. Each block of $Dup(r.MID, 2^{p+k})$ is 2^{p+k} bits long. From the proof of Theorem 4.1 it follows that there is a block in $Dup(r.MID, 2^{p+k})$ so that the robots have an agreement in direction in the rounds corresponding to that block. Recall that the robots simulate the MEETING algorithm from Section 3.2.0.1 in the rounds corresponding to

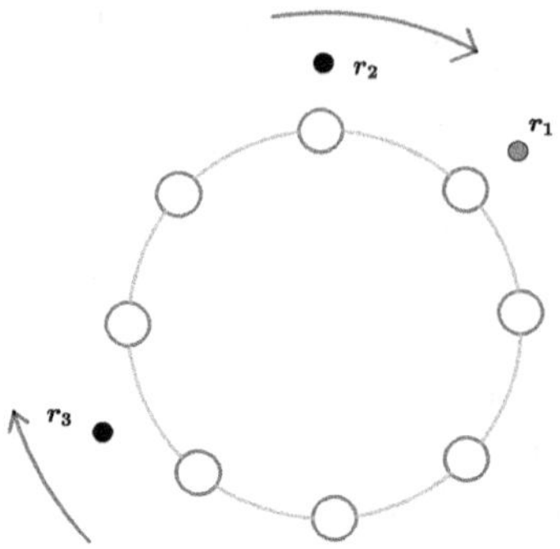

Figure 4.2: The robots meeting for the first time in without chirality setting

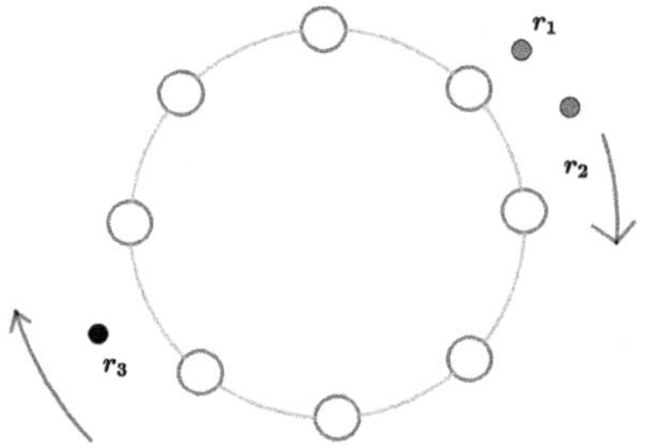

Figure 4.3: The robots agreeing on a common direction

each block. Hence it follows from Theorem 3.1 that two robots are guaranteed to meet during the rounds corresponding to the aforesaid block. Therefore, the algorithm ensures that the meeting takes place within $2^k \left(\frac{k(k-1)}{2} + k + 1\right) \sum_{i=0}^{p} 2^i < k^2 2^{k+\lceil \log n \rceil + 3}$ rounds. □

4.4 Exploration with Termination by robots without Chirality

For simplicity, assume that the robots are placed arbitrarily at distinct nodes of the ring. We shall remove this assumption at the end of this section. Initially the *state* variable of all three robots are set to `search`. We shall adopt a strategy similar to the one used in Section 3.2.0.2. In fact, we only need to make some modifications in the algorithms to be executed by the robots with *state* `search` and `settled`.

The robots will execute the MEETING algorithm described in Section 4.3 until another robot is encountered. The robots will keep count of the number of rounds since the beginning in the variable *STime*. Now by Theorem 4.2, two of the robots are guaranteed to meet within $k^2 2^{k+\lceil \log n \rceil+3}$ rounds. Upon meeting, the robots will agree on a common direction, say the right direction of the robot with larger ID, refer to Figure . Without loss of generality, assume that the agreed direction is the clockwise direction. The robot with smaller ID, say r_1, will become the `settled` robot and the one with larger ID, say r_2, will continue moving in the clockwise direction. The robot r_1 will save the port number leading to the agreed direction, i.e., clockwise. Let r_3 denote the third robot which is still executing the MEETING algorithm. It can be shown (see Section 4.4.1) that a second meeting is guaranteed to take place on or before $(\lceil \log 2n \rceil + 1)$th phase, i.e., within $k^2 2^{k+\lceil \log n \rceil+4}$ rounds from the start of the algorithm. Recall that in Section 3.2.0.2 where the robots had chirality, the second meeting took place either between r_2 and r_3, or between r_3 and r_1, refer to Figure 4.5 and 4.6. However, in the current setting where the robots do not have chirality, the second meeting may also take place between r_1 and r_2. This is because r_3 is moving in clockwise direction in some rounds and counterclockwise in other rounds. Hence there is a possibility that r_2 and r_3 may swap over an edge and r_1 meets r_2 first, refer to Figure 4.4. However, even then it is not difficult to show (see Section 4.4.1) that r_3 is guaranteed to meet r_1 or r_2 , on or before $(\lceil \log 2n \rceil + 1)$th phase i.e., within $k^2 2^{k+\lceil \log n \rceil+4}$ rounds from the start of the algorithm.

Now consider the following cases depending on which of the two robots meet on the second meeting.

1. Suppose that the second meeting takes place between r_1 and r_2. In this case the ring has been explored and r_2 finds out n and informs r_1 about it. Then r_2 will continue moving in the clockwise direction. Both robots will terminate after the round when $STime = k^2 2^{k+\lceil \log n \rceil+4}$. Recall that

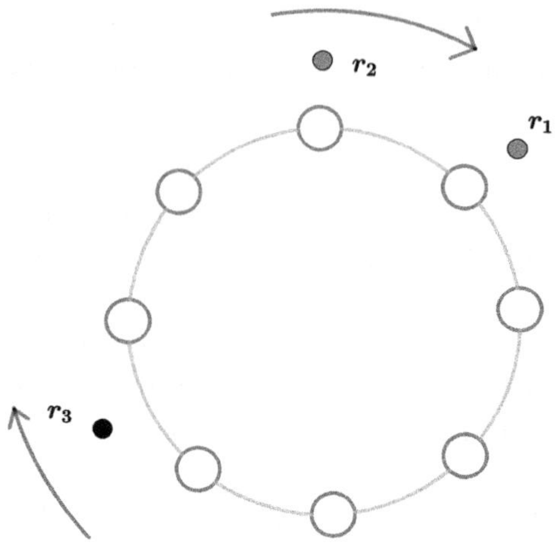

Figure 4.4: The first case of second meeting.

r_3 is guaranteed to meet one of them in the meantime and will terminate immediately.

2. Suppose that the second meeting takes place between r_2 and r_3. Then r_2 informs r_3 about the agreed direction. Hence the case reduces to the setting of Section 3.2. Therefore r_2 and r_3 will change their *state* to `forward` and `bounce` respectively and execute the algorithms as before.

3. Now suppose that the second meeting takes place between r_1 and r_3. In this case r_3 will come to know about the agreed direction and again the case reduces to the setting of Section 3.2. So r_3 will continue to move in the agreed direction i.e., clockwise.

It follows from the above discussions that the robots will terminate after exploring the ring within $k^2 2^{k+\lceil \log n \rceil + 4} + 23n = O(n)$ rounds.

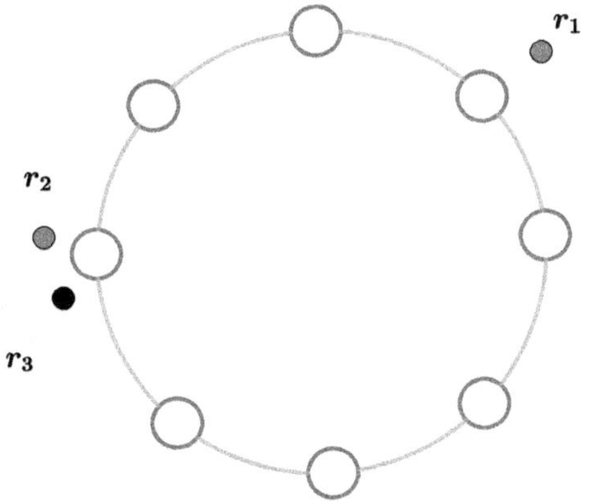

Figure 4.5: The second case of second meeting, subcase 1.

4.4.1 The Main Results

From the discussions in the above subsection and Theorem 4.1 and Theorem 4.2, we get the following result,

Theorem 4.3. EXPLORATION *with explicit termination is solvable by three robots without chirality in* $k^2 2^{k+\lceil \log n \rceil+4} + 23n = O(n)$ *rounds.*

Proof. The robots will execute the MEETING algorithm described in Section 4.3 until another robot is encountered. By Theorem 4.2, two of the robots are guaranteed to meet within $k^2 2^{k+\lceil \log n \rceil+3}$ rounds. Upon meeting, the robots will agree on a common direction, say the clockwise direction. The robot with smaller ID, say r_1, will become the `settled` robot and the one with larger ID, say r_2, will continue moving in the clockwise direction. Let r_3 denote the third robot which is still executing the MEETING algorithm. Observe that r_2 and r_3 will try to move in the same direction for some $4n$ consecutive rounds in the $(\lceil \log 2n \rceil + 1) = \lceil \log 4n \rceil$th phase. Within the first $2n$ rounds a meeting should take place by Lemma 3.1. If this meeting involves r_3 then we are done. Otherwise r_1 and r_2 meet each other and then by again applying by Lemma 3.1, r_3 will meet one of them within the following $2n$ rounds.

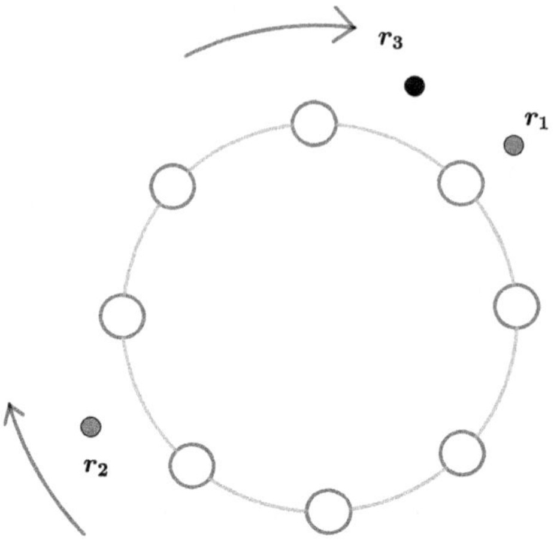

Figure 4.6: The second case of second meeting, subcase 2.

Now there are three cases depending on which of the two robots meet on the second meeting: the second meeting takes place between r_1 and r_2 (Case 1), the second meeting takes place between r_2 and r_3 (Case 2) and the second meeting takes place between r_1 and r_3 (Case 3). It follows from the discussions in Section 4.4 that the robots will terminate after exploring the ring within $k^2 2^{k+\lceil \log n \rceil +4} + 23n = O(n)$ rounds.

□

Recall that we assumed that the robots are placed initially at distinct nodes of the ring. We now show that this assumption is not necessary if the initial configuration has two robots r_1, r_2 at the same node and the third robot r_3 at a different node. Then the case reduces to the situation when the first meeting takes place. Then r_1 and r_2 will change their *state* to `settled` and `forward` while r_3 will execute the MEETING algorithm with *state* `search`. The algorithm will progress as before and achieve exploration with termination.

If all three robots are in the same node in the initial configuration then the three robots will compare their identifiers and will change their *state* to `settled`, `forward` and `bounce` accordingly. Again, the algorithm will progress as before and achieve exploration with termination.

4.5 Concluding Remarks

In this chapter, we showed that EXPLORATION (with explicit termination) in a dynamic always connected ring without any landmark node is solvable by three non-anonymous robots without chirality. This is optimal in terms of the number of robots used as the problem is known to be unsolvable by two robots. Our algorithm takes $O(k^2 2^k n)$ rounds to solve the problem where n is the size of the ring and k is the length of the identifiers of the robots. An interesting question is whether the problem can be solved in $O(poly(k)n)$ rounds. However with $k = O(1)$ the round complexity is $O(n)$. This is asymptotically optimal as there are n nodes to be explored and in each round three robots can visit at most three nodes. A challenging problem that remains open is EXPLORATION in a dynamic network of arbitrary underlying topology. Except for some bounds on the number of robots obtained in the recent work [50], almost nothing is known.

Chapter 5

The Computational Landscape of Autonomous Mobile Robots: The Visibility Perspective

5.1 Introduction

In this chapter, we consider *robots* to be *autonomous*, *anonymous*, *identical*, *homogenous* and moving and operating in the Euclidean plane. The robots are viewed as points and they operate according to the traditional *Look-Compute-Move* (*LCM*) cycles in synchronous rounds. In *Look* phase robots take a snapshot of the space, in the *Compute* phase the robots execute its algorithm using the snapshot as input, then move to the computed destination in *Move* phase. The robots are collectively able to perform some tasks and solve some problems.

In recent times, exhaustive investigation has also been done [17, 44] about the issues of *memory persistence* and *communication capability*, have on the solvability of a problem and computational capability of a system. In light of these facts, four models have been identified and investigated, $\mathcal{OBLOT}$, $\mathcal{LUMI}$, $\mathcal{FSTA}$ and $\mathcal{FCOM}$.

In the most common model $\mathcal{OBLOT}$, in the addition to standard assumptions of *anonymity* and *uniformity*, the robots are *silent*, i.e., without explicit means of communication, and *oblivious*, i.e., they have no persistent memory to record information of previous cycles.

The other model which is generally considered as antithesis to $\mathcal{OBLOT}$ model, is the $\mathcal{LUMI}$ model first formally defined in [25, 26], where the robots have both persistent memory and communication, although it must be noted that the remembering or communicating can be done only in limited capacity, i.e., the robots can remember or communicate finite number of bits.

Two new models have been introduced in [43] by eliminating one of the two capabilities of $\mathcal{LUMI}$ model, in each case. These two models are $\mathcal{FSTA}$ and $\mathcal{FCOM}$. In $\mathcal{FSTA}$ model the communication capability is absent while in $\mathcal{FCOM}$ model the robots do not have persistent memory. In [44] these models have been considered to investigate the question *is it better to remember or to communicate*?.

In this work we consider another factor, i.e., *visibility*, which helps to investigate the matter from a different angle and is of interest from both theoretical and practical point of view. If $\mathcal{M}$ denotes a model and σ is a scheduler then traditionally $\mathcal{M}^\sigma$ denotes a model $\mathcal{M}$ under scheduler σ. Here $\mathcal{M} \in \{\mathcal{OBLOT}, \mathcal{FSTA}, \mathcal{FCOM}, \mathcal{LUMI}\}$ and $\sigma \in \{FSYNCH, SSYNCH\}$. We here define $\mathcal{M_V}^\sigma$ denotes a model $\mathcal{M}$ under scheduler σ and visibility state $\mathcal{V}$. Here $\mathcal{V} \in \{\mathcal{F.V.}, \mathcal{L.V.}\}$. Here $\mathcal{F.V.}$ denotes the full visibility model and $\mathcal{L.V.}$ denotes the limited visibility model. In limited visibility model, each robot can view upto a constant radius of their position and the initial visibility graph is connected.

All the works done till now had given the full visibility power to the robots. So we try to answer a number of questions,

- Does restriction on visibility have no significant impact whatsoever on the computational power of a model? In other words, is any problem which is solvable in full visibility model, solvable in limited visibility model also?

- If the answer to the second question mentioned above is no, then can the impairment be *always* adjusted by minor adjustments, i.e., by keeping the model intact but by making the scheduler more powerful?

- If the answer to the above question is also no, then what are the cases where the lack of full visibility can be compensated? Can all the cases be classified?

We have shown the answer to the first question is no, e.g., we have proved that $\mathcal{FSTA}^{\mathcal{F}}_{\mathcal{L.V.}} < \mathcal{FSTA}^{\mathcal{F}}_{\mathcal{F.V.}}$. This result turns out to be true for all the four models $\{\mathcal{OBLOT}, \mathcal{FSTA}, \mathcal{FCOM}, \mathcal{LUMI}\}$. After we got answer to our first question, we tried to answer our second question. A definite answer to the second question shall give us some insight about whether any one of the two parameters of *visibility* and *synchronicity* have any precedence over the other. But as we shall see this does not happen. For e.g., we got the result that $\mathcal{FCOM}^{\mathcal{F}}_{\mathcal{L.V.}} \perp \mathcal{FCOM}^{\mathcal{S}}_{\mathcal{F.V.}}$, which effectively shows that both the capabilities are important, and deficiency in one of the parameter cannot be compensated by making the other parameter stronger. In the process, we have defined a new problem *EqOsc* which we have shown to be unsolvable unless the scheduler is fully synchronous, but solvable if the scheduler is fully synchronous, even under limited visibility in $\mathcal{FSTA}$ and $\mathcal{FCOM}$ models. The third question as of now, yet remains unanswered, and subject to further investigations.

The results presented in this chapter gives a whole new insight to the parameter of visibility and its relevance relative to the parameter of synchronicity, one that requires exhaustive analysis, even beyond the amount of investigation that had been done in this chapter.

Investigations regarding the computational power of robots under synchronous schedulers was done by the authors Flocchini et. al. in [44]. Main focus of the investigation in this work was which of the two capabilities was more important: *persistent memory* or *communication*. In the course of their investigation they proved that under fully synchronous scheduler communication is more powerful than persistent memory. In addition to that, they gave a complete exhaustive map of the relationships among models and schedulers.

In [17], the previous work of characterizing the relations between the robot models and three type of schedulers was continued. The authors provided a more refined map of the computational landscape for robots operating under fully synchronous and semi-synchronous schedulers, by removing the assumptions on robots' movements of *rigidity* and common *chirality*. Further authors establish some preliminary results with respect to asynchronous scheduler.

The previous two works considered that the robots was assumed to have unlimited amounts of energy. In [18], the authors removed this assumption and started the study of computational capabilities of robots whose energy is limited, albeit renewable. In these systems, the activated entities uses all its energy to execute an LCM cycle and then the energy is restored after a period of inactivity. They studied the impact that memory persistence and communication capabilities have on the computational power of such robots by analyzing the computational relationship between the four models $\{\mathcal{OBLOT}, \mathcal{FSTA}, \mathcal{FCOM}, \mathcal{LUMI}\}$ under the energy constraint. They provided a full characterization of this relationship. Among the many results they proved that for energy-constrained robots, $\mathcal{FCOM}$ is more powerful than $\mathcal{FSTA}$.

In all the three above mentioned works, the robots had full visibility. A robot uses its visibility power in the *Look* phase of the LCM cycle to acquire information about its surroundings, i.e., position and lights (if any) of other robots. The biggest drawback of full visibility assumption is that it is not practically feasible. So, recently some of the authors [7, 41, 49, 87] have considered limited visibility. For example, in [41] they considered that the robots can see up to a fixed radius V from it. So it was important to study the power of different robot models under limited visibility.

The rest of the chapter is organized as follows, in Section 5.2, we describe the contributions in the chapter in brief. In Section 5.3, we describe the model and associated definitions in brief. In Section 5.4, we describe the ANGLE EQUALIZATION PROBLEM and in Section 5.5 we compare the power of *visibility* and *synchronicity* by introducing the EQUIVALENT OSCILLATION PROBLEM.

5.2 Our Contributions

Let $\mathcal{M}_{\mathcal{V}}^{\mathcal{X}}$ denote a model $\mathcal{M}$ under scheduler $\mathcal{X}$ with visibility $\mathcal{V}$. Here $\mathcal{M} \in \{\mathcal{OBLOT}, \mathcal{FSTA}, \mathcal{FCOM}, \mathcal{LUMI}\}$, $\mathcal{X} \in \{\mathcal{F}, \mathcal{S}\}$, here $\mathcal{F}$ and $\mathcal{S}$ denotes $FSYNCH$ and $SSYNCH$ schedulers respectively, and $\mathcal{V} \in \{\mathcal{F.V.}, \mathcal{L.V.}\}$. $\mathcal{A}_{\mathcal{C}}^{\mathcal{B}} \geq \mathcal{D}_{\mathcal{F}}^{\mathcal{E}}$ denotes that the model $\mathcal{A}$, under scheduler $\mathcal{B}$ and visibility $\mathcal{C}$ is computationally not weaker than the model $\mathcal{D}$ under scheduler $\mathcal{E}$ and visibility $\mathcal{F}$, $\mathcal{A}_{\mathcal{C}}^{\mathcal{B}} > \mathcal{D}_{\mathcal{F}}^{\mathcal{E}}$ denotes that the model $\mathcal{A}$ under scheduler $\mathcal{B}$ and visibility $\mathcal{C}$ is computationally more powerful than the model $\mathcal{D}$ under scheduler $\mathcal{E}$ and visibility $\mathcal{F}$, $\mathcal{A}_{\mathcal{C}}^{\mathcal{B}} \equiv \mathcal{D}_{\mathcal{F}}^{\mathcal{E}}$ denotes that the model $\mathcal{A}$ under scheduler $\mathcal{B}$ and visibility $\mathcal{C}$ is computationally equivalent to the model $\mathcal{D}$ under scheduler $\mathcal{E}$ and visibility $\mathcal{F}$ and $\mathcal{A}_{\mathcal{C}}^{\mathcal{B}} \perp \mathcal{D}_{\mathcal{F}}^{\mathcal{E}}$ denotes that the model $\mathcal{A}$ under scheduler $\mathcal{B}$ and visibility $\mathcal{C}$ is computationally incomparable with the model $\mathcal{D}$ under scheduler $\mathcal{E}$ and visibility $\mathcal{F}$.

We first examine the computational relationship under a constant model and scheduler between limited and full visibility conditions. We find that in both fully synchronous and semi-synchronous cases, a model under full visibility is strictly more powerful than a model under limited visibility. We get the following results:

1. $\mathcal{OBLOT}_{\mathcal{F.V.}}^{\mathcal{F}} > \mathcal{OBLOT}_{\mathcal{L.V.}}^{\mathcal{F}}$
2. $\mathcal{FSTA}_{\mathcal{F.V.}}^{\mathcal{F}} > \mathcal{FSTA}_{\mathcal{L.V.}}^{\mathcal{F}}$
3. $\mathcal{FCOM}_{\mathcal{F.V.}}^{\mathcal{F}} > \mathcal{FCOM}_{\mathcal{L.V.}}^{\mathcal{F}}$
4. $\mathcal{LUMI}_{\mathcal{F.V.}}^{\mathcal{F}} > \mathcal{LUMI}_{\mathcal{L.V.}}^{\mathcal{F}}$
5. $\mathcal{OBLOT}_{\mathcal{F.V.}}^{\mathcal{S}} > \mathcal{OBLOT}_{\mathcal{L.V.}}^{\mathcal{S}}$
6. $\mathcal{FSTA}_{\mathcal{F.V.}}^{\mathcal{S}} > \mathcal{FSTA}_{\mathcal{L.V.}}^{\mathcal{S}}$
7. $\mathcal{FCOM}_{\mathcal{F.V.}}^{\mathcal{S}} > \mathcal{FCOM}_{\mathcal{L.V.}}^{\mathcal{S}}$
8. $\mathcal{LUMI}_{\mathcal{F.V.}}^{\mathcal{S}} > \mathcal{LUMI}_{\mathcal{L.V.}}^{\mathcal{S}}$

Next step is examining the computational relationship between the four models under consideration, namely, $\{\mathcal{OBLOT}, \mathcal{FSTA}, \mathcal{FCOM}, \mathcal{LUMI}\}$ under limited visibility between fully synchronous and semi-synchronous schedulers. We find that under limited visibility conditions each of the three models are more powerful under fully synchronous scheduler.

9. $\mathcal{OBLOT}^{\mathcal{F}}_{\mathcal{L.V.}} > \mathcal{OBLOT}^{\mathcal{S}}_{\mathcal{L.V.}}$

10. $\mathcal{FSTA}^{\mathcal{F}}_{\mathcal{L.V.}} > \mathcal{FSTA}^{\mathcal{S}}_{\mathcal{L.V.}}$

11. $\mathcal{FCOM}^{\mathcal{F}}_{\mathcal{L.V.}} > \mathcal{FCOM}^{\mathcal{S}}_{\mathcal{L.V.}}$

12. $\mathcal{LUMI}^{\mathcal{F}}_{\mathcal{L.V.}} > \mathcal{LUMI}^{\mathcal{S}}_{\mathcal{L.V.}}$

Together with the three results mentioned immediately above, we also get an idea which of the capabilities, *visibility* or *synchronicity* is more powerful. From the previous results we generally conclude that $\mathcal{M}^{\mathcal{S}}_{\mathcal{L.V.}} < \mathcal{M}^{\mathcal{S}}_{\mathcal{F.V.}}$ and $\mathcal{M}^{\mathcal{S}}_{\mathcal{L.V.}} < \mathcal{M}^{\mathcal{F}}_{\mathcal{L.V.}}$. If we can prove that $\mathcal{M}^{\mathcal{F}}_{\mathcal{L.V.}} \geq \mathcal{M}^{\mathcal{S}}_{\mathcal{F.V.}}$, then it shall imply that by making the scheduler stronger, the limitation in visibility can be compensated. Similarly if we can prove that $\mathcal{M}^{\mathcal{S}}_{\mathcal{F.V.}} \geq \mathcal{M}^{\mathcal{F}}_{\mathcal{L.V.}}$, then it shall imply that by giving complete visibility, the weakness in terms of scheduler can be compensated. But after our detailed investigation it has been revealed that neither of the above cases happen and in general $\mathcal{M}^{\mathcal{F}}_{\mathcal{L.V.}} \perp \mathcal{M}^{\mathcal{S}}_{\mathcal{F.V.}}$. Specifically the results are:

13. $\mathcal{OBLOT}^{\mathcal{F}}_{\mathcal{L.V.}} \perp \mathcal{OBLOT}^{\mathcal{S}}_{\mathcal{F.V.}}$

14. $\mathcal{FSTA}^{\mathcal{F}}_{\mathcal{L.V.}} \perp \mathcal{FSTA}^{\mathcal{S}}_{\mathcal{F.V.}}$

15. $\mathcal{FCOM}^{\mathcal{F}}_{\mathcal{L.V.}} \perp \mathcal{FCOM}^{\mathcal{S}}_{\mathcal{F.V.}}$

16. $\mathcal{LUMI}^{\mathcal{F}}_{\mathcal{L.V.}} \perp \mathcal{LUMI}^{\mathcal{S}}_{\mathcal{F.V.}}$

5.3 Model and Definitions

In this section, we shall present a formal description of the model. Then we mention some definitions and notations that will be used throughout the chapter.

5.3.1 The Basics

In this chapter we consider a team $R = \{r_0, \ldots, r_n\}$ of computational entities moving and operating in the Euclidean Plane $\mathbb{R}^2$, which are viewed as points and called *robots*. The robots can move freely and continuously in the plane. Each robot has its own local coordinate system and it always perceives itself at its origin; there might not be consistency between these coordinate systems. The robots are *identical*: they are indistinguishable by their appearance and they execute the same protocol, and they are *autonomous*, i.e., without any central control.

The robots operate in *Look – Compute – Move* (*LCM*) cycles. When activated a robot executes a cycle by performing the following three operations:

1. *Look*: The robots activate its sensors to obtain a snapshot of the positions occupied by the robots according to its co-ordinate system.

2. *Compute*: The robot executes its algorithm using the snapshot as input. The result of the computation is a destination point.

3. *Move*: The robot moves to the computed destination. If the destination is the current location, the robot stays still.

All robots are initially idle. The amount of time to complete a cycle is assumed to be finite, and the *Look* is assumed to be instantaneous. The robots may not have any agreement in terms of their local coordinate system. By *chirality*, we mean the robots agree on the same circular orientation of the plane, or in other words they agree on "clockwise" direction. In our chapter, we do not assume the robots to have a common sense of chirality.

5.3.2 The Computational Models

There are four basic robot models which are considered in literature, they are namely, $\{\mathcal{OBLOT}, \mathcal{FSTA}, \mathcal{FCOM}, \mathcal{LUMI}\}$.

In the most common model, $\mathcal{OBLOT}$, the robots are *silent*: they have no explicit means of communication; furthermore they are *oblivious*: at the start of the cycle, a robot has no memory of observations and computations performed in previous cycles.

In the next common model, $\mathcal{LUMI}$, each robot r is equipped with a persistent visible state variable $Light[r]$, called *light*, whose values are taken from a finite set C of states called *colors* (including the color that represents the initial state when the light is off). The colors of the lights can be set in each cycle by r at the end of its *Compute* operation. A light is *persistent* from one computational cycle to the next: the color is not automatically reset at the end of a cycle; the robots are otherwise oblivious, forgetting all other information from previous cycles. In $\mathcal{LUMI}$, the *Look* operation produces a colored snapshot; i.e., it returns the set of pairs (*position*, *color*) of the robots. Note that if $|C| = 1$, then the light is not used; this case corresponds to the $\mathcal{OBLOT}$ model.

It is sometimes convenient to describe a robot r as having $k \geq 1$ lights, denoted $r.light_1, \ldots, r.light_k$, where the values of $r.light_i$ are from a finite set of colors C_i, and to consider $Light[r]$ as a k-tuple of variables; clearly, this corresponds to r having a single light that uses $\prod_{i=1}^{k} |C_i|$ colors.

The lights provide simultaneously persistent memory and direct means of communication, although both limited to a constant number of bits per cycle. Two sub-models of $\mathcal{LUMI}$ have been defined and investigated , each offering only one of these two capabilities.

In the first model, $\mathcal{FSTA}$, a robot can only see the color of its own light; that is, the light is an *internal* one and its color merely encodes an internal state. Hence the robots are *silent*, as in $\mathcal{OBLOT}$, but are *finite-state*. Observe that a snapshot in $\mathcal{FSTA}$ is same as in $\mathcal{OBLOT}$.

In the second model, $\mathcal{FCOM}$, the lights *external*: a robot can communicate to the other robots through its colored light but forgets the color of its own light by the next cycle; that is, robots are *finite-communication* but are *oblivious*. A snapshot in $\mathcal{FCOM}$ is like in $\mathcal{LUMI}$ except that, for the position x where the robot r performing the *Look* is located, $Light[r]$ is omitted from the set of colors present at x.

In all the above models, a *configuration* $C(t)$ at time t is the multi-set of the n pairs of the (x), where c_i is the color of robot r_i at time t.

5.3.3 The Schedulers

With respect to the activation schedule of the robots, and the duration of their *Look-Compute-Move* cycles, the fundamental distinction is between the *asynchronous* and *synchronous* settings.

In the *asynchronous* setting (ASYNCH), there is no common notion of time, each robot is activated independently of others, the duration of each phase is finite but unpredictable and might be different cycles.

In the *synchronous* setting (SSYNCH), also called semi-synchronous, time is divided into discrete intervals, called *rounds*; in each round some robots are activated simultaneously, and perform their *LCM* cycle in perfect synchronization.

A popular synchronous setting which plays an important role is the *fully-synchronous* setting (FSYNCH) where every robot is activated in every round; the is, the activation scheduler has no adversarial power.

In all two settings, the selection of which robots are activated at a round is made by an adversarial *scheduler*, whose only limit is that every robot must be activated infinitely often (i.e., it is fair scheduler). In the following, for all synchronous schedulers, we use round and time interchangeably.

5.3.4 The Visibility Models

In our work we do comparative analysis of computational models with robots having *full* and *limited* visibility. In *full visibility* model, denoted as $\mathcal{F}.\mathcal{V}.$, the robots have sensorial devices that allows it to observe the positions of the other robots in its local co-ordinate system.

In *limited visibility* model, denoted as $\mathcal{L}.\mathcal{V}.$, a robot can only observe upto a fixed distance V_r from it. Suppose, $r_p(t)$ denote the position of a robot r at the beginning of round t. Then we define the circle with center at $r_p(t)$ and radius V_r to be the *Circle of Visibility* of r at round t. Here the radius V_r is same for all the robots. The result of *Look* operation in round t will be the position of the robots and lights(if any) of the robots inside the circle of visibility.

We now define the *Visibility Graph*, $G = (V, E)$ of a configuration. Let C be a given configuration. Then all the robot positions become the vertices of G and we say an edge exists between any two vertices if and only if the robots present there can see each other.

The necessary condition for the problems we have defined in the chapter is that the *Visibility Graph* of the initial configuration must be connected.

5.3.5 Some important definitions

We define our computational relationships similar to that of [44]. Let $\mathcal{M} = \{\mathcal{OBLOT}, \mathcal{FSTA}, \mathcal{FCOM}, \mathcal{LUMI}\}$ be the robot models under investigation, the set of activation schedulers be $\mathcal{S} = \{FSYNCH, ASYNCH\}$ and the set of visibility models be $\mathcal{V} = \{\mathcal{F}.\mathcal{V}., \mathcal{L}.\mathcal{V}.\}$.

We denote by $\mathcal{R}$ the set of all teams of robots satisfying the core assumptions (i.e., they are identical, autonomous, and operate in LCM cycles), and $R \in \mathcal{R}$ a team of robots having identical capabilities (e.g., common coordinate system, persistent storage, internal identity, rigid movements etc.). By $\mathcal{R}_n \subset R$ we denote the set of all teams of size n.

By *problem* we mean a task where a fixed number of robots have to form some configuration or configurations (which may be a function of time) subject to some conditions, within a finite amount of time.

Given a model $M \in \mathcal{M}$, a scheduler $S \in \mathcal{S}$, visibility $V \in \mathcal{V}$, and a team of robots $R \in \mathcal{R}$, let $Task(M, S, V; R)$ denote the set of problems solvable by R in M, with visibility V and under adversarial scheduler S.

Let M, $N \in \mathcal{M}$, S_1, $S_2 \in \mathcal{S}$ and V_1, $V_2 \in \mathcal{V}$. We define the relationships between model M with visibility V_1 under scheduler S_1 and model N with visibility V_2 under scheduler S_2:

- *computationally not less powerful* ($M_{V_1}^{S_1} \geq N_{V_2}^{S_2}$), if $\forall\ R \in \mathcal{R}$ we have $Task(M, S_1; R) \supseteq Task(N, S_2; R)$;
- *computationally more powerful* ($M_{V_1}^{S_1} > N_{V_2}^{S_2}$), if $M_{V_1}^{S_1} \geq N_{V_2}^{S_2}$ and $\exists R \in \mathcal{R}$ such that $Task(M, S_1, V_1; R) \setminus Task(N, S_2, V_2; R) \neq \emptyset$;
- *computationally equivalent* ($M_{V_1}^{S_1} \equiv N_{V_2}^{S_2}$), if $M_{V_1}^{S_1} \geq N_{V_2}^{S_2}$ and $M_{V_1}^{S_1} \leq N_{V_2}^{S_2}$;
- *computationally orthogonal or incomparable*, ($M_{V_1}^{S_1} \perp N_{V_2}^{S_2}$), if $\exists R_1, R_2 \in \mathcal{R}$ such that $Task(M, S_1, V_1; R_1) \setminus Task(N, S_2, V_2; R_1) \neq \emptyset$ and $Task(N, S_2, V_2; R_2) \setminus Task(M, S_1, V_1; R_2) \neq \emptyset$.

For simplicity of notation, for a model $M \in \mathcal{M}$, let M^F and M^S denote M^{Fsynch} and M^{Ssynch}, respectively; and let $M_V^F(R)$ and $M_V^S(R)$ denote $Task(M, FSYNCH, V; R)$ and $Task(M, SSYNCH, V; R)$, respectively.

5.3.6 Some Fundamental Comparisons

Trivially,

1. $\mathcal{LUMI} \geq \mathcal{FSTA} \geq \mathcal{OBLOT}$ and $\mathcal{LUMI} \geq \mathcal{FCOM} \geq \mathcal{OBLOT}$, when the $Visibility$ and *Synchronicity* is fixed.
2. $\mathcal{FSYNCH} \geq \mathcal{SSYNCH} \geq \mathcal{ASYNCH}$ when the model and $Visibility$ is fixed.
3. $\mathcal{F.V.} \geq \mathcal{L.V.}$ when the model and *Synchronicity* is fixed.

5.4 ANGLE EQUALIZATION PROBLEM

In this section, we shall define a problem to show the limitation of limited visibility over full visibility even when the model is very powerful. Our main motivation here is to investigate whether restriction on visibility have any significant impact whatsoever on the computational power of a model or not.

Definition 5.1. ***Problem Angle Equalization (AE)****: Suppose four robots r_1, r_2, r_3 and r_4 are placed in positions A, B, C and D respectively, as given in Configuration (I). The line AB makes an acute angle θ_1 with BC and the line CD makes an acute θ_2 with BC. Here $\theta_1 < \theta_2 < 90°$.*

The robots must form the Configuration (II) without any collision. The robots r_2 and r_3 must remain fixed in their positions.

5.4.1 Algorithm for AE problem in $\mathcal{OBLOT}^{S}_{\mathcal{F}.\mathcal{V}}$

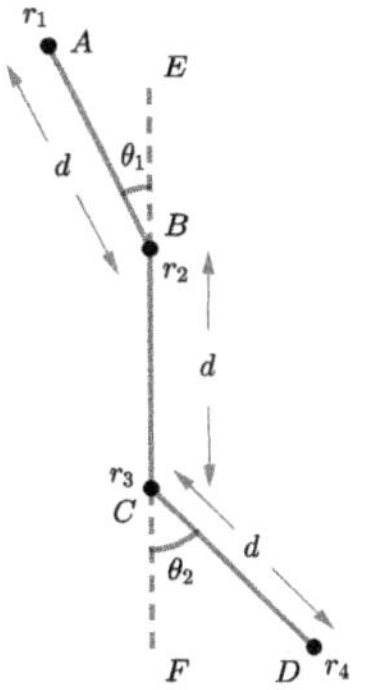

Figure 5.1: Configuration (I) of Problem AE

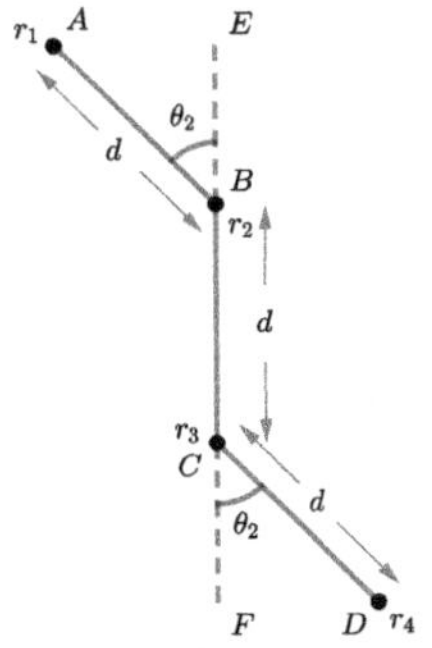

Figure 5.2: Configuration (II) of Problem AE

Under full visibility conditions, each robot can see all the robot locations in the plane. Now each robot can uniquely identify its position in the plane. Therefore whenever the robot r_1 is activated, it will move to the position A' such that the $\angle A'BE = \theta_2$. The rest of the robots will not move. After the robot r_1 moves

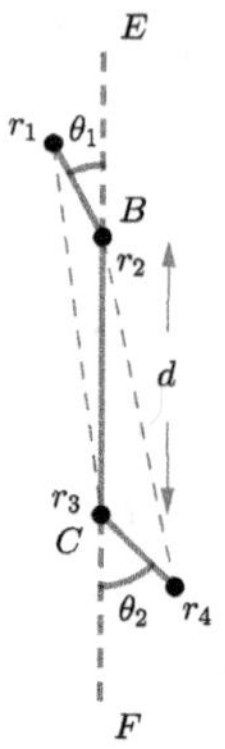

Figure 5.3: Visibility Range Gap

all the robots can perceive that Configuration (II) is obtained and henceforward there will be no further movement of the robots. Hence the problem is solved.

Lemma 5.1. $\forall\ R \in \mathcal{R}_4$, $AE \in \mathcal{OBLOT}^{\mathcal{S}}_{\mathcal{F}.\mathcal{V}}$.

Corollary 5.0.1. $\forall\ R \in \mathcal{R}_4$, $AE \in \mathcal{OBLOT}^{\mathcal{F}}_{\mathcal{F}.\mathcal{V}}$.

Proof. Follows from Lemma 5.1. □

Corollary 5.0.2. $\forall\ R \in \mathcal{R}_4$, $AE \in \mathcal{FSTA}^{\mathcal{S}}_{\mathcal{F}.\mathcal{V}}$.

Proof. Follows from Lemma 5.1. □

Corollary 5.0.3. $\forall\ R \in \mathcal{R}_4$, $AE \in \mathcal{FSTA}^{\mathcal{F}}_{\mathcal{F}.\mathcal{V}}$.

Proof. Follows from Corollary 5.0.1. □

Corollary 5.0.4. $\forall\ R \in \mathcal{R}_4$, $AE \in \mathcal{FCOM}^{\mathcal{S}}_{\mathcal{F}.\mathcal{V}}$.

Proof. Follows from Lemma 5.1. □

Corollary 5.0.5. $\forall\ R \in \mathcal{R}_4$, $AE \in \mathcal{FCOM}^{\mathcal{F}}_{\mathcal{F}.\mathcal{V}}$.

Proof. Follows from Corollary 5.0.1. □

Corollary 5.0.6. $\forall\ R \in \mathcal{R}_4,\ AE \in \mathcal{LUMI}^{\mathcal{S}}_{\mathcal{F}.\mathcal{V}}$.

Proof. Follows from Lemma 5.1. □

Corollary 5.0.7. $\forall\ R \in \mathcal{R}_4,\ AE \in \mathcal{LUMI}^{\mathcal{F}}_{\mathcal{F}.\mathcal{V}}$.

Proof. Follows from Corollary 5.0.1. □

5.4.2 Impossibility of Solving AE Problem in Limited Visibility Model

Lemma 5.2. $\exists\ R \in \mathcal{R}_4,\ AE \notin \mathcal{LUMI}^{\mathcal{F}}_{\mathcal{L}.\mathcal{V}.}$.

Proof. Let there exists an Algorithm $\mathcal{A}$ to solve the problem in $\mathcal{LUMI}^{\mathcal{F}}_{\mathcal{L}.\mathcal{V}.}$. If Configuration (II) has to be formed from Configuration (I) then the robot r_1 must know the value of the angle it has to form. If r_1 has to move to the position A' such that the $\angle A'BE = \theta_2$, then the robot r_1 must know the position of two robots r_3 and r_4 respectively in the initial configuration, i.e., the positions C and D respectively. Unless the position C is known, the robot r_1 cannot perceive that it has to form the angle with respect to the extended line of the line segment. And unless it knows the position D, it cannot perceive the value θ_2 that it has to form. But if $V_r = BC + \epsilon$, then it is not possible for the robot r_1 to see them from the initial configuration. Also according the requirement of the problem the robots r_2 and r_3 cannot move. Therefore to solve the problem r_1 must move. Now, if r_1 has to move, unless r_1 performs the required move to form Configuration (II) in one move, it has to move preserving the angle θ_1. This is because r_1 does not know the fact that $\theta_1 < \theta_2$. The argument holds for r_4. And we have already seen that the initial configuration does not give the required information to form Configuration (II) in one move.

Now the only way the robot r_1 can move preserving the angle, is by moving along the line segment AB. Now note that if r_1 reaches B, the angle becomes 0. Also as collisions are not allowed the robot r_1 cannot cross B. Similarly, the robot r_3 can only move along line segment CD and it cannot cross the position

C. Now, by moving along the line segments AB and CD respectively, however much the two robots r_1 and r_4 may come closer to B and C respectively, the adversary may choose the value of ϵ in such a way that the position C is outside the visibility range of r_1 and B is outside the visibility range of r_2, refer to Figure 5.3. Note that the robots r_2 and r_3 cannot see r_4 and r_1 respectively, therefore it is also unknown to them which robot should perform the required move to form Configuration (II). Though r_2 and r_3 can measure the angles θ_1 and θ_2 respectively. It is not possible to store the value of the angles with finite number of lights. Hence the problem cannot be solved. □

From Lemma 5.2 follows:

Corollary 5.0.8. $\exists\ R \in \mathcal{R}_4,\ AE \notin \mathcal{LUMI}^{\mathcal{S}}_{\mathcal{L.V}}.$

Corollary 5.0.9. $\exists\ R \in \mathcal{R}_4,\ AE \notin \mathcal{FSTA}^{\mathcal{F}}_{\mathcal{L.V}}.$

Corollary 5.0.10. $\exists\ R \in \mathcal{R}_4,\ AE \notin \mathcal{FSTA}^{\mathcal{S}}_{\mathcal{L.V}}.$

Proof. Follows from Corollary 5.0.8 □

Corollary 5.0.11. $\exists\ R \in \mathcal{R}_4,\ AE \notin \mathcal{FCOM}^{\mathcal{F}}_{\mathcal{L.V}}.$

Corollary 5.0.12. $\exists\ R \in \mathcal{R}_4,\ AE \notin \mathcal{FCOM}^{\mathcal{S}}_{\mathcal{L.V}}.$

Proof. Follows from Corollary 5.0.8 □

Corollary 5.0.13. $\exists\ R \in \mathcal{R}_4,\ AE \notin \mathcal{OBLOT}^{\mathcal{F}}_{\mathcal{L.V}}.$

Corollary 5.0.14. $\exists\ R \in \mathcal{R}_4,\ AE \notin \mathcal{OBLOT}^{\mathcal{S}}_{\mathcal{L.V}}.$

Proof. Follows from Corollary 5.0.8 □

We get the following results:

Theorem 5.1. $\mathcal{OBLOT}^{\mathcal{F}}_{\mathcal{F.V}} > \mathcal{OBLOT}^{\mathcal{F}}_{\mathcal{L.V}}.$

Proof. From Corollary 5.0.1 and Corollary 5.0.13. □

Theorem 5.2. $\mathcal{OBLOT}^{\mathcal{S}}_{\mathcal{F}.\mathcal{V}.} > \mathcal{OBLOT}^{\mathcal{S}}_{\mathcal{L}.\mathcal{V}.}$

Proof. From Lemma 5.1 and Corollary 5.0.14. □

Theorem 5.3. $\mathcal{FSTA}^{\mathcal{F}}_{\mathcal{F}.\mathcal{V}.} > \mathcal{FSTA}^{\mathcal{F}}_{\mathcal{L}.\mathcal{V}.}$

Proof. From Corollary 5.0.3 and Corollary 5.0.9. □

Theorem 5.4. $\mathcal{FSTA}^{\mathcal{S}}_{\mathcal{F}.\mathcal{V}.} > \mathcal{FSTA}^{\mathcal{S}}_{\mathcal{L}.\mathcal{V}.}$

Proof. From Corollary 5.0.2 and Corollary 5.0.10. □

Theorem 5.5. $\mathcal{FCOM}^{\mathcal{F}}_{\mathcal{F}.\mathcal{V}.} > \mathcal{FCOM}^{\mathcal{F}}_{\mathcal{L}.\mathcal{V}.}$

Proof. From Corollary 5.0.5 and Corollary 5.0.11. □

Theorem 5.6. $\mathcal{FCOM}^{\mathcal{S}}_{\mathcal{F}.\mathcal{V}.} > \mathcal{FCOM}^{\mathcal{S}}_{\mathcal{L}.\mathcal{V}.}$

Proof. From Corollary 5.0.4 and Corollary 5.0.12. □

Theorem 5.7. $\mathcal{LUMI}^{\mathcal{F}}_{\mathcal{F}.\mathcal{V}.} > \mathcal{LUMI}^{\mathcal{F}}_{\mathcal{L}.\mathcal{V}.}$

Proof. From Corollary 5.0.7 and Lemma 5.2. □

Theorem 5.8. $\mathcal{LUMI}^{\mathcal{S}}_{\mathcal{F}.\mathcal{V}.} > \mathcal{LUMI}^{\mathcal{S}}_{\mathcal{L}.\mathcal{V}.}$

Proof. From Corollary 5.0.6 and Corollary 5.0.8. □

5.5 EQUIVALENT OSCILLATION PROBLEM

After we have seen the amount of impact *Visibility* has on the computational power of a model, the next natural question that comes to one's mind is that whether the deficiency in the visibility can be compensated by making some other parameter stronger. We particularly choose the parameter of *Synchronicity* and see whether synchronicity can compensate limited visibility.

Definition 5.2. ***Problem Equivalent Oscillation (EqOsc)***: *Let three robots r_1, r_2 and r_3 be initially placed at three points B, A and C respectively. $AB = AC = d$. Let B', C' be points collinear on the line such that $AB' = AC' = \frac{2d}{3}$. The robots r_1 and r_3 have to change their positions from B to B' and back to B, C to C' and back to C respectively, while always being equidistant from r_2, i.e., A (Equidistant Condition).*

More formally speaking, if there is a round t such that the robots r_1 and r_3 is at B and C respectively, then there must must exist a round $t' > t$, such that r_1 and r_3 is at B' and C' respectively. Similarly if at round t', r_1 and r_3 is at B' and C' respectively, then there must exist a round $t'' > t'$, such that r_1 and r_3 is at B and C respectively (Oscillation Condition).

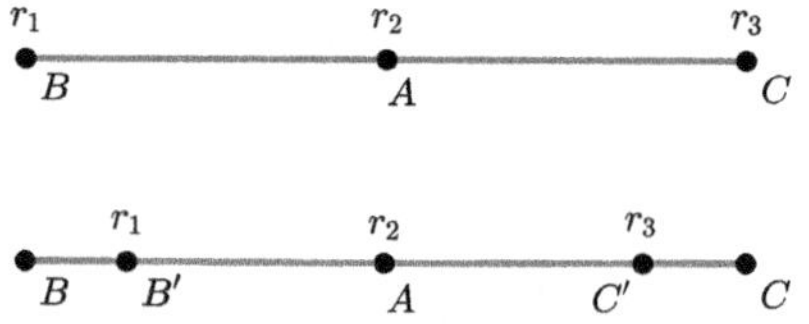

Figure 5.4: Illustration of *EqOsc* problem

We prove that this problem is not solvable in $\mathcal{LUMI}^{S}_{\mathcal{F}.\mathcal{V}.}$.

Lemma 5.3. $\exists\, R \in \mathcal{R}_3$, $EqOsc \notin \mathcal{LUMI}^{S}_{\mathcal{F}.\mathcal{V}.}$.

Proof. Let the the robots r_1, r_3 be able to successfully execute the movements satisfying the conditions of the problem till round t. Let at the beginning of round $t+1$ the robots r_1 and r_3 be at the points B and C respectively. So next the robots r_1 and r_3 must move to the points B', C' respectively. Note that the robots must move together or otherwise the equidistant condition is not satisfied. From round $t+1$ we activate only one of the terminal robots alternatively. Let at rounds $t+1$, $t+3$, $t+5$,......., the robot r_1 is activated and let at rounds $t+2$, $t+4$, $t+6$,......, the robot r_3 is activated.

Now whenever r_1 or r_3 makes a movement(when they are activated) the equidistant condition is violated. If neither r_1 nor r_3 makes any movement indefinitely then the oscillating condition is violated.

The problem cannot be solved in $\mathcal{LUMI}^{\mathcal{S}}_{\mathcal{F}.\mathcal{V}.}$.

□

From Lemma 5.3 following result naturally follows,

Corollary 5.8.1. *$\exists\ R \in \mathcal{R}_3$, $EqOsc \notin \mathcal{FSTA}^{\mathcal{S}}_{\mathcal{F}.\mathcal{V}.}$ and, $\exists\ R \in \mathcal{R}_3$, $EqOsc \notin \mathcal{FCOM}^{\mathcal{S}}_{\mathcal{F}.\mathcal{V}.}$.*

5.5.1 Solution of problem Equivalent Oscillation in $\mathcal{FSTA}^{\mathcal{F}}_{\mathcal{L}.\mathcal{V}.}$

We now give an algorithm to solve the problem in $\mathcal{FSTA}^{\mathcal{F}}_{\mathcal{L}.\mathcal{V}.}$. The pseudocode of the algorithm is given below.

Algorithm 11: Algorithm $AlgEOSTA$ for Problem EqOsc executed by each robot r in $\mathcal{FSTA}^{\mathcal{F}}_{\mathcal{L}.\mathcal{V}.}$

```
d = distance from the closer robot;
A = Position of the middle robot;
if not a terminal robot then
    Remain static
else
    if Light = Off or Light = F then
        Light ← N
        Move to a point D on the line segment such that AD = 2d/3
    else
        Light ← F
        Move to a point D on the line segment such that AD = 3d/2
```

Description and Correctness of $AlgEOSTA$ Let the three robots r_1, r_2 and r_3 be at B, A, and C respectively. Here $V_r > AB$, and $V_r > AC$, but $V_r < BC$. So there are three robots among which there is one robot which can see two other robots except itself, we call this robot the *middle robot*. The other two robots can see only one other robot except itself. We call each of these two robots *terminal robot*. The terminal robots are initially at a distance D from the middle robot. Whenever a robot is activated it can understand whether it is a terminal or a middle robot. Now, each of the robots save a light which is initially saved to Off. If a robot perceives that it is a middle robot it does not do anything. If it is a terminal robot and its light is set to Off or F, it changes its light to N and moves closer a distance two-third of the present distance from the middle robot, and if its light is set to N, it changes its light to F and moves further to a distance 1.5 times of the present distance from the middle robot. As we consider a fully synchronous system both the terminal robots execute the nearer and further movement alternatively together, and hence our problem is solved.

Hence we get the following result:

Lemma 5.4. $\forall\ R \in \mathcal{R}_3$, $EqOsc \in \mathcal{FSTA}^{\mathcal{F}}_{\mathcal{L.V.}}$.

Theorem 5.9. $\mathcal{FSTA}^{\mathcal{F}}_{\mathcal{L.V.}} > \mathcal{FSTA}^{\mathcal{S}}_{\mathcal{L.V.}}$

Proof. By Corollary 5.8.1 the problem cannot be solved in $\mathcal{FSTA}^{\mathcal{S}}_{\mathcal{L.V.}}$, and, trivially $\mathcal{FSTA}^{\mathcal{F}}_{\mathcal{L.V.}} \geq \mathcal{FSTA}^{\mathcal{S}}_{\mathcal{L.V.}}$.

□

Theorem 5.10. $\mathcal{FSTA}^{\mathcal{F}}_{\mathcal{L.V.}} \perp \mathcal{FSTA}^{\mathcal{S}}_{\mathcal{F.V.}}$

Proof. By Corollary 5.8.1 and Lemma 5.4, $EqOsc$ cannot be solved in $\mathcal{FSTA}^{\mathcal{S}}_{\mathcal{F.V.}}$ but can be solved in $\mathcal{FSTA}^{\mathcal{F}}_{\mathcal{L.V.}}$.

Similarly, by Corollary 5.0.9 and 5.0.2 AE cannot be solved in $\mathcal{FSTA}^{\mathcal{F}}_{\mathcal{L.V.}}$ but can be solved in $\mathcal{FSTA}^{\mathcal{S}}_{\mathcal{F.V.}}$. Hence the result.

□

5.5.2 Solution of problem Equivalent Oscillation in $\mathcal{FCOM}^{\mathcal{F}}_{\mathcal{L.V.}}$

We now give an algorithm to solve the problem in $\mathcal{FCOM}^{\mathcal{F}}_{\mathcal{L.V.}}$. The pseudocode of the algorithm is given below.

Algorithm 12: Algorithm *AlgEOCOM* for Problem EqOsc executed by each robot r in $\mathcal{FCOM}^{\mathcal{F}}_{\mathcal{L.V}}$.

```
d = distance from the closer robot;
A = Position of the middle robot;
if not a terminal robot then
    Remain static
    if Visible light = NIL or FAR then
        Light ← FAR
    else if Visible light = NEAR then
        Light ← NEAR
else
    if Visible light = NIL or Visible light = NEAR then
        Light ← NEAR
        Move to a point D on the line segment such that AD = 2d/3
    else if Visible light = FAR then
        Light ← FAR
        Move to a point D on the line segment such that AD = 3d/2
```

Description and Correctness of *AlgEOCOM* Let the three robots r_1, r_2 and r_3 be at B, A, and C respectively. Here $V_r > AB$, and $V_r > AC$, but $V_r < BC$. So there are three robots among which there is one robot which can see two other robots except itself, we call this robot the *middle robot*. The other two robots can see only one other robot except itself. We call each of these two robots *terminal robot*. Whenever a robot is activated it can understand whether it is a terminal or a middle robot. Now, each of the robots has a light which is initially saved to NIL. If a robot perceives that it is a middle robot it can see the lights of the two terminal robots. If it perceives the lights of the terminal robots to be set to NIL or FAR, it sets its own light to FAR. And if it perceives the lights of the terminal robots to be set to $NEAR$, it sets its own light to $NEAR$. The middle robot only changes its light but does not change its position. If it is a terminal robot it can only see the light of the middle robot. If the light of the middle robot is set to NIL or $NEAR$, the terminal robot changes its light to $NEAR$ and moves closer to a distance which is two-third of the present distance from the middle robot. And if the light of the middle robot is set to FAR, it changes its light to FAR and moves away to a distance 1.5 times the present distance from the middle robot. As we consider a fully synchronous system both the terminal robots execute the nearer and further movement alternatively together, and hence our problem is solved.

Hence we get the following result:

Lemma 5.5. $\forall\ R \in \mathcal{R}_3$, $EqOsc \in \mathcal{FCOM}^{\mathcal{F}}_{\mathcal{L}.\mathcal{V}.}$.

Theorem 5.11. $\mathcal{FCOM}^{\mathcal{F}}_{\mathcal{L}.\mathcal{V}.} > \mathcal{FCOM}^{\mathcal{S}}_{\mathcal{L}.\mathcal{V}.}$

Proof. By Corollary 5.8.1 the problem cannot be solved in $\mathcal{FCOM}^{\mathcal{S}}_{\mathcal{L}.\mathcal{V}.}$, and, trivially $\mathcal{FCOM}^{\mathcal{F}}_{\mathcal{L}.\mathcal{V}.} \geq \mathcal{FCOM}^{\mathcal{S}}_{\mathcal{L}.\mathcal{V}.}$. Hence our theorem. □

Theorem 5.12. $\mathcal{FCOM}^{\mathcal{F}}_{\mathcal{L}.\mathcal{V}.} \perp \mathcal{FCOM}^{\mathcal{S}}_{\mathcal{F}.\mathcal{V}.}$

Proof. By Corollary 5.8.1 and Lemma 5.5, $EqOsc$ cannot be solved in $\mathcal{FCOM}^{\mathcal{S}}_{\mathcal{F}.\mathcal{V}.}$ but can be solved in $\mathcal{FCOM}^{\mathcal{F}}_{\mathcal{L}.\mathcal{V}.}$.

Similarly, by Corollary 5.0.11 and 5.0.4 AE cannot be solved in $\mathcal{FCOM}^{\mathcal{F}}_{\mathcal{L}.\mathcal{V}.}$ but can be solved in $\mathcal{FCOM}^{\mathcal{S}}_{\mathcal{F}.\mathcal{V}.}$. Hence the result.

□

5.5.3 Similar deductions in $\mathcal{OBLOT}$ and $\mathcal{LUMI}$

Theorem 5.13. $\mathcal{OBLOT}^{\mathcal{F}}_{\mathcal{L}.\mathcal{V}.} \perp \mathcal{OBLOT}^{\mathcal{S}}_{\mathcal{F}.\mathcal{V}.}$

Proof. We have proved that the problem AE cannot be solved in $\mathcal{OBLOT}^{\mathcal{F}}_{\mathcal{L}.\mathcal{V}.}$ but can be solved in $\mathcal{OBLOT}^{\mathcal{S}}_{\mathcal{F}.\mathcal{V}.}$.

Now we consider the problem *Rendezvous* which was proved to be impossible in $\mathcal{OBLOT}^{\mathcal{S}}_{\mathcal{F}.\mathcal{V}.}$ in [99]. Now we claim that in our model the problem is possible to solve in $\mathcal{OBLOT}^{\mathcal{F}}_{\mathcal{L}.\mathcal{V}.}$. This is because in our model we assume the visibility graph of the robots in the initial configuration to be connected. Now when there are only two robots in the initial configuration this means, all the robots in the initial configuration can see each other. Hence in this case the problem reduces to $\mathcal{OBLOT}^{\mathcal{F}}$ model. Now it is well known that *rendezvous* problem is solvable in this model, as the robots just move to the mid-point of the line segment joining them. Hence the result.

□

Theorem 5.14. $\mathcal{OBLOT}^{\mathcal{F}}_{\mathcal{L}.\mathcal{V}} > \mathcal{OBLOT}^{\mathcal{S}}_{\mathcal{L}.\mathcal{V}.}$

Proof. Trivially $\mathcal{OBLOT}^{\mathcal{F}}_{\mathcal{L}.\mathcal{V}} \geq \mathcal{OBLOT}^{\mathcal{S}}_{\mathcal{L}.\mathcal{V}.}$ and by Theorem 5.13 the problem *Rendezvous* is solvable in $\mathcal{OBLOT}^{\mathcal{F}}_{\mathcal{L}.\mathcal{V}}$ but not in $\mathcal{OBLOT}^{\mathcal{S}}_{\mathcal{L}.\mathcal{V}.}$.

□

Lemma 5.6. $\forall\ R \in \mathcal{R}_3$, $EqOsc \in \mathcal{LUMI}^{\mathcal{F}}_{\mathcal{L}.\mathcal{V}.}$.

Proof. From Lemma 5.4 and 5.5. □

Theorem 5.15. $\mathcal{LUMI}^{\mathcal{F}}_{\mathcal{L}.\mathcal{V}.} \perp \mathcal{LUMI}^{\mathcal{S}}_{\mathcal{F}.\mathcal{V}.}$

Proof. By Lemma 5.2 and Corollary 5.0.7 the problem AE cannot be solved in $\mathcal{LUMI}^{\mathcal{F}}_{\mathcal{L}.\mathcal{V}.}$ but can be solved in $\mathcal{LUMI}^{\mathcal{S}}_{\mathcal{F}.\mathcal{V}.}$.

By Lemma 5.3 and 5.6 , the problem $EqOsc$ cannot be solved in $\mathcal{LUMI}^{\mathcal{S}}_{\mathcal{F}.\mathcal{V}.}$ but can be solved in $\mathcal{LUMI}^{\mathcal{F}}_{\mathcal{L}.\mathcal{V}.}$. Hence, the result.

□

Theorem 5.16. $\mathcal{LUMI}^{\mathcal{F}}_{\mathcal{L}.\mathcal{V}} > \mathcal{LUMI}^{\mathcal{S}}_{\mathcal{L}.\mathcal{V}.}$

Proof. Trivially $\mathcal{LUMI}^{\mathcal{F}}_{\mathcal{L}.\mathcal{V}} \geq \mathcal{LUMI}^{\mathcal{S}}_{\mathcal{L}.\mathcal{V}.}$ and by Lemma 5.6 and Lemma 5.3 the problem $EqOsc$ is solvable in $\mathcal{LUMI}^{\mathcal{F}}_{\mathcal{L}.\mathcal{V}}$ but not in $\mathcal{LUMI}^{\mathcal{S}}_{\mathcal{L}.\mathcal{V}.}$.

□

5.6 Concluding Remarks

We have initiated the analysis of computational capabilities of mobile robots having limited visibility. The models $\{\mathcal{OBLOT}, \mathcal{FSTA}, \mathcal{FCOM}, \mathcal{LUMI}\}$ have been considered by us, and we have more or less exhaustively analyzed the possible relationships when the model is fixed.

Chapter 6

Conclusion

In this chapter, we conclude the thesis by subsuming all the technical results from the previous chapters and also highlight some interesting directions for future research.

In Chapter 2, we studied the DISPERSION problem on arbitrary graphs with anonymous robots. We have presented a memory optimal randomized algorithm for DISPERSION from rooted configuration by anonymous robots. This resolves an open problem posed in [80]. Time complexity of our algorithm is $\Theta(k^2)$ rounds in the worst case. Any algorithm that solves the problem requires $\Omega(k)$ rounds in the worst case. To see this, consider a path with $n \geq k$ nodes with all robots initially at one of its one degree nodes. An interesting open problem is to close this gap.

Open Problem 1. *Give an algorithm for* DISPERSION *from rooted configuration, which requires* $\Omega(k)$ *rounds, or, improve the time lower bound to* $\Omega(k^2)$.

For arbitrary configurations, the random walk based algorithm presented has been presented in [80] but it requires the robots to stay active indefinitely. Therefore an interesting open question is whether it is possible to solve the problem by anonymous robots from non-rooted configurations without requiring robots to stay active indefinitely.

Open Problem 2. *Give an algorithm for* DISPERSION *from arbitrary configu-*

ration, where the robots eventually terminate and which requires $O(\log \Delta)$ bits of memory at each robot.

In Chapter 3 and Chapter 4, we considered the EXPLORATION problem. In Chapter 3 we considered the problem in the chirality and Chapter 4 we removed the assumption of chirality. We showed that EXPLORATION (with explicit termination) in a dynamic always connected ring without any landmark node is solvable by three non-anonymous robots without chirality. This is optimal in terms of the number of robots used as the problem is known to be unsolvable by two robots. Our algorithm takes $O(k^2 2^k n)$ rounds to solve the problem where n is the size of the ring and k is the length of the identifiers of the robots. An interesting question is whether the problem can be solved in $O(poly(k)n)$ rounds.

Open Problem 3. *Give an algorithm for* EXPLORATION *in a dynamic ring, which requires $O(poly(k)n)$ rounds, k is the length of the identifiers of the robots.*

However with $k = O(1)$ the round complexity is $O(n)$. This is asymptotically optimal as there are n nodes to be explored and in each round three robots can visit at most three nodes. A challenging problem that remains open is EXPLORATION in a dynamic network of arbitrary underlying topology. Except for some bounds on the number of robots obtained in the recent work [50], almost nothing is known.

Open Problem 4. *Investigate the problem of* EXPLORATION *in a dynamic network of arbitrary underlying topology..*

In Chapter 5, we have analysed computational capabilities of mobile robots having limited visibility under fully synchronous and semi-synchronous schedulers. We have considered all the four models $\{\mathcal{OBLOT}, \mathcal{FSTA}, \mathcal{FCOM}, \mathcal{LUMI}\}$, and we have more or less exhaustively analyzed the possible relationships when the model is fixed. But a huge amount of interesting questions still remains to be solved. The possible future directions are outlined in the following two open problems.

Open Problem 5. *Investigate the cross-model relationships under limited visibility conditions.*

Open Problem 6. *Investigate the computational relationships when the scheduler is asynchronous.*

Bibliography

[1] Ercan U Acar, Howie Choset, Yangang Zhang, and Mark Schervish. Path planning for robotic demining: Robust sensor-based coverage of unstructured environments and probabilistic methods. *The International journal of robotics research*, 22(7-8):441–466, 2003.

[2] Ranendu Adhikary, Kaustav Bose, Manash Kumar Kundu, and Buddhadeb Sau. Mutual visibility by asynchronous robots on infinite grid. In *Algorithms for Sensor Systems: 14th International Symposium on Algorithms and Experiments for Wireless Sensor Networks, ALGOSENSORS 2018, Helsinki, Finland, August 23–24, 2018, Revised Selected Papers 14*, pages 83–101. Springer, 2019.

[3] Ankush Agarwalla, John Augustine, William K. Moses Jr., Madhav Sankar K., and Arvind Krishna Sridhar. Deterministic dispersion of mobile robots in dynamic rings. In Paolo Bellavista and Vijay K. Garg, editors, *Proceedings of the 19th International Conference on Distributed Computing and Networking, ICDCN 2018, Varanasi, India, January 4-7, 2018*, pages 19:1–19:4. ACM, 2018. doi:10.1145/3154273.3154294.

[4] Chrysovalandis Agathangelou, Chryssis Georgiou, and Marios Mavronicolas. A distributed algorithm for gathering many fat mobile robots in the plane. In *Proceedings of the 2013 ACM symposium on Principles of distributed computing*, pages 250–259. ACM, 2013.

[5] Susanne Albers and Monika Rauch Henzinger. Exploring unknown environments. *SIAM J. Comput.*, 29(4):1164–1188, 2000. doi:10.1137/S009753979732428X.

[6] Aisha Aljohani and Gokarna Sharma. Complete visibility for mobile robots with lights tolerating faults. *International Journal of Networking and Computing*, 8(1):32–52, 2018.

[7] Hideki Ando, Yoshinobu Oasa, Ichiro Suzuki, and Masafumi Yamashita. Distributed memoryless point convergence algorithm for mobile robots with limited visibility. *IEEE Transactions on Robotics and Automation*, 15(5):818–828, 1999. doi: 10.1109/70.795787.

[8] Ronald C Arkin. Motor schema—based mobile robot navigation. *The International journal of robotics research*, 8(4):92–112, 1989.

[9] John Augustine and William K. Moses Jr. Dispersion of mobile robots: A study of memory-time trade-offs. In *Proceedings of the 19th International Conference on Distributed Computing and Networking, ICDCN 2018, Varanasi, India, January 4-7, 2018*, pages 1:1–1:10, 2018. doi: 10.1145/3154273.3154293.

[10] Tucker Balch and Ronald C Arkin. Behavior-based formation control for multirobot teams. *IEEE transactions on robotics and automation*, 14(6):926–939, 1998.

[11] Alethea Barbaro, Baldvin Einarsson, Björn Birnir, Sven Sigursson, Héinn Valdimarsson, Ólafur Karvel Pálsson, Sveinn Sveinbjörnsson, and orsteinn Sigursson. Modelling and simulations of the migration of pelagic fish. *ICES Journal of Marine Science*, 66(5):826–838, 2009.

[12] Subhash Bhagat and Krishnendu Mukhopadhyaya. Optimum circle formation by autonomous robots. *Advanced Computing and Systems for Security: Volume Five*, pages 153–165, 2018.

[13] Kaustav Bose, Ranendu Adhikary, Sruti Gan Chaudhuri, and Buddhadeb Sau. Crash tolerant gathering on grid by asynchronous oblivious robots. *arXiv preprint arXiv:1709.00877*, 2017.

[14] Kaustav Bose, Ranendu Adhikary, Manash Kumar Kundu, and Buddhadeb Sau. Arbitrary pattern formation on infinite grid by asynchronous oblivious robots. *Theoretical Computer Science*, 815:213–227, 2020.

[15] Kaustav Bose, Manash Kumar Kundu, Ranendu Adhikary, and Buddhadeb Sau. Arbitrary pattern formation by asynchronous opaque robots with lights. In *Structural Information and Communication Complexity - 26th International Colloquium, SIROCCO 2019, L'Aquila, Italy, July 1-4, 2019, Proceedings*, pages 109–123, 2019. doi: 10.1007/978-3-030-24922-9_8.

[16] Marjorie Bournat, Swan Dubois, and Franck Petit. Gracefully degrading gathering in dynamic rings. In *20th International Symposium on Stabilization, Safety, and Security of Distributed Systems, SSS 2018, Tokyo, Japan, November 4-7, 2018, Proceedings*, volume 11201 of *Lecture Notes in Computer Science*, pages 349–364. Springer, 2018. doi:10.1007/978-3-030-03232-6_23.

[17] Kevin Buchin, Paola Flocchini, Irina Kostitsyna, Tom Peters, Nicola Santoro, and Koichi Wada. Autonomous mobile robots: Refining the computational landscape. In *IEEE International Parallel and Distributed Processing Symposium Workshops, IPDPS Workshops 2021, Portland, OR, USA, June 17-21, 2021*, pages 576–585. IEEE, 2021. doi:10.1109/IPDPSW52791.2021.00091.

[18] Kevin Buchin, Paola Flocchini, Irina Kostitsyna, Tom Peters, Nicola Santoro, and Koichi Wada. On the computational power of energy-constrained mobile robots: Algorithms and cross-model analysis. In Merav Parter, editor, *Structural Information and Communication Complexity - 29th International Colloquium, SIROCCO 2022, Paderborn, Germany, June 27-29, 2022, Proceedings*, volume 13298 of *Lecture Notes in Computer Science*, pages 42–61. Springer, 2022. doi:10.1007/978-3-031-09993-9_3.

[19] Francesco Bullo, Jorge Cortés, and Sonia Martinez. *Distributed control of robotic networks: a mathematical approach to motion coordination algorithms*, volume 27. Princeton University Press, 2009.

[20] Arnaud Casteigts, Paola Flocchini, Walter Quattrociocchi, and Nicola Santoro. Time-varying graphs and dynamic networks. *Int. J. Parallel Emergent Distributed Syst.*, 27(5):387–408, 2012. doi:10.1080/17445760.2012.668546.

[21] Serafino Cicerone, Gabriele Di Stefano, and Alfredo Navarra. Asynchronous arbitrary pattern formation: the effects of a rigorous approach. *Distributed Computing*, 32:91–132, 2019.

[22] Mark Cieliebak, Paola Flocchini, Giuseppe Prencipe, and Nicola Santoro. Distributed computing by mobile robots: Gathering. *SIAM Journal on Computing*, 41(4):829–879, 2012.

[23] Gianlorenzo D'Angelo, Gabriele Di Stefano, Ralf Klasing, and Alfredo Navarra. Gathering of robots on anonymous grids and trees without multiplicity detection. *Theoretical Computer Science*, 610:158–168, 2016. doi:10.1016/j.tcs.2014.06.045.

[24] Shantanu Das, Paola Flocchini, Shay Kutten, Amiya Nayak, and Nicola Santoro. Map construction of unknown graphs by multiple agents. *Theor. Comput. Sci.*, 385(1-3):34–48, 2007. doi:10.1016/j.tcs.2007.05.011.

[25] Shantanu Das, Paola Flocchini, Giuseppe Prencipe, Nicola Santoro, and Masafumi Yamashita. The power of lights: Synchronizing asynchronous robots using visible bits. In *2012 IEEE 32nd International Conference on Distributed Computing Systems, Macau, China, June 18-21, 2012*, pages 506–515. IEEE Computer Society, 2012. doi:10.1109/ICDCS.2012.71.

[26] Shantanu Das, Paola Flocchini, Giuseppe Prencipe, Nicola Santoro, and Masafumi Yamashita. Autonomous mobile robots with lights. *Theor. Comput. Sci.*, 609:171–184, 2016. doi:10.1016/j.tcs.2015.09.018.

[27] Shantanu Das, Giuseppe Antonio Di Luna, and Leszek Antoni Gasieniec. Patrolling on dynamic ring networks. In *45th International Conference on Current Trends in Theory and Practice of Computer Science, SOFSEM 2019, Nový Smokovec, Slovakia, January 27-30, 2019, Proceedings*, volume 11376 of *Lecture Notes in Computer Science*, pages 150–163. Springer, 2019. doi:10.1007/978-3-030-10801-4_13.

[28] Xavier Défago and Akihiko Konagaya. Circle formation for oblivious anonymous mobile robots with no common sense of orientation. In *Proceedings of the second ACM international workshop on Principles of mobile computing*, pages 97–104, 2002.

[29] Xavier Défago and Samia Souissi. Non-uniform circle formation algorithm for oblivious mobile robots with convergence toward uniformity. *Theoretical Computer Science*, 396(1-3):97–112, 2008.

[30] Xiaotie Deng and Christos H. Papadimitriou. Exploring an unknown graph. *J. Graph Theory*, 32(3):265–297, 1999.

[31] Aditya Milind Deshpande, Rumit Kumar, Mohammadreza Radmanesh, Nalini Veerabhadrappa, Manish Kumar, and Ali A Minai. Self-organized circle formation around an unknown target by a multi-robot swarm using a local communication strategy. In *2018 Annual American Control Conference (ACC)*, pages 4409–4413. IEEE, 2018.

[32] Giuseppe Antonio Di Luna, Paola Flocchini, Federico Poloni, Nicola Santoro, and Giovanni Viglietta. The mutual visibility problem for oblivious robots. In *CCCG*, 2014.

[33] Gabriele Di Stefano and Alfredo Navarra. Gathering of oblivious robots on infinite grids with minimum traveled distance. *Information and Computation*, 254:377–391, 2017. doi:10.1016/j.ic.2016.09.004.

[34] Yoann Dieudonné and Andrzej Pelc. Deterministic network exploration by anonymous silent agents with local traffic reports. *ACM Trans. Algorithms*, 11(2):10:1–10:29, 2014. doi:10.1145/2594581.

[35] Ayan Dutta, Sruti Gan Chaudhuri, Suparno Datta, and Krishnendu Mukhopadhyaya. Circle formation by asynchronous fat robots with limited visibility. In *Distributed Computing and Internet Technology: 8th International Conference, ICDCIT 2012, Bhubaneswar, India, February 2-4, 2012. Proceedings 8*, pages 83–93. Springer, 2012.

[36] Thomas Erlebach, Michael Hoffmann, and Frank Kammer. On temporal graph exploration. In *42nd International Colloquium on Automata, Languages, and Programming, ICALP 2015, Kyoto, Japan, July 6-10, 2015, Proceedings, Part I*, volume 9134 of *Lecture Notes in Computer Science*, pages 444–455. Springer, 2015. doi:10.1007/978-3-662-47672-7_36.

[37] Caterina Feletti, Carlo Mereghetti, and Beatrice Palano. Uniform circle formation for swarms of opaque robots with lights. In *Stabilization, Safety, and Security of Distributed Systems: 20th International Symposium, SSS 2018, Tokyo, Japan, November 4–7, 2018, Proceedings 20*, pages 317–332. Springer, 2018.

[38] Matthias Fischer, Daniel Jung, and Friedhelm Meyer auf der Heide. Gathering anonymous, oblivious robots on a grid. In *International Symposium on Algorithms and Experiments for Sensor Systems, Wireless Networks and Distributed Robotics*, pages 168–181. Springer, 2017. doi:10.1007/978-3-319-72751-6_13.

[39] Paola Flocchini, Bernard Mans, and Nicola Santoro. On the exploration of time-varying networks. *Theor. Comput. Sci.*, 469:53–68, 2013. doi:10.1016/j.tcs.2012.10.029.

[40] Paola Flocchini, Giuseppe Prencipe, and Nicola Santoro. Self-deployment algorithms for mobile sensors on a ring. In *Algorithmic Aspects of Wireless Sensor Networks: Second International Workshop, ALGOSENSORS 2006, Venice, Italy, July 15, 2006, Revised Selected Papers 2*, pages 59–70. Springer, 2006.

[41] Paola Flocchini, Giuseppe Prencipe, Nicola Santoro, and Peter Widmayer. Gathering of asynchronous robots with limited visibility. *Theor. Comput. Sci.*, 337(1-3):147–168, 2005. doi:10.1016/j.tcs.2005.01.001.

[42] Paola Flocchini, Giuseppe Prencipe, Nicola Santoro, and Peter Widmayer. Arbitrary pattern formation by asynchronous, anonymous, oblivious robots. *Theoretical Computer Science*, 407(1-3):412–447, 2008.

[43] Paola Flocchini, Nicola Santoro, Giovanni Viglietta, and Masafumi Yamashita. Rendezvous with constant memory. *Theor. Comput. Sci.*, 621:57–72, 2016. doi:10.1016/j.tcs.2016.01.025.

[44] Paola Flocchini, Nicola Santoro, and Koichi Wada. On memory, communication, and synchronous schedulers when moving and computing. In Pascal Felber, Roy Friedman, Seth Gilbert, and Avery Miller, editors, *23rd International Conference on Principles of Distributed Systems, OPODIS 2019, December 17-19, 2019, Neuchâtel, Switzerland*, volume 153 of *LIPIcs*, pages 25:1–25:17. Schloss Dagstuhl - Leibniz-Zentrum für Informatik, 2019. doi:10.4230/LIPIcs.OPODIS.2019.25.

[45] Pierre Fraigniaud, David Ilcinkas, Guy Peer, Andrzej Pelc, and David Peleg. Graph exploration by a finite automaton. *Theor. Comput. Sci.*, 345(2-3):331–344, 2005. doi:10.1016/j.tcs.2005.07.014.

[46] Emilio Frazzoli, Francesco Bullo, Jorge Cortés, and Sonia Martinez. On synchronous robotic networks-part ii: Time complexity of rendezvous and deployment algorithms. *IEEE Transactions on Automatic Control*, 52(12):2214–2226, 2007.

[47] Jakob Fredslund and Maja J Mataric. A general algorithm for robot formations using local sensing and minimal communication. *IEEE transactions on robotics and automation*, 18(5):837–846, 2002.

[48] Barun Gorain, Partha Sarathi Mandal, Kaushik Mondal, and Supantha Pandit. Collaborative dispersion by silent robots. In *International Sym-*

posium on Stabilizing, Safety, and Security of Distributed Systems, pages 254–269. Springer, 2022.

[49] Pritam Goswami, Avisek Sharma, Satakshi Ghosh, and Buddhadeb Sau. Time optimal gathering of myopic robots on an infinite triangular grid. In Stéphane Devismes, Franck Petit, Karine Altisen, Giuseppe Antonio Di Luna, and Antonio Fernández Anta, editors, *Stabilization, Safety, and Security of Distributed Systems - 24th International Symposium, SSS 2022, Clermont-Ferrand, France, November 15-17, 2022, Proceedings*, volume 13751 of *Lecture Notes in Computer Science*, pages 270–284. Springer, 2022. doi:10.1007/978-3-031-21017-4_18.

[50] Tsuyoshi Gotoh, Paola Flocchini, Toshimitsu Masuzawa, and Nicola Santoro. Exploration of dynamic networks: Tight bounds on the number of agents. *Journal of Computer and System Sciences*, 122:1–18, 2021. doi:10.1016/j.jcss.2021.04.003.

[51] Tsuyoshi Gotoh, Yuichi Sudo, Fukuhito Ooshita, Hirotsugu Kakugawa, and Toshimitsu Masuzawa. Group exploration of dynamic tori. In *38th IEEE International Conference on Distributed Computing Systems, ICDCS 2018, Vienna, Austria, July 2-6, 2018*, pages 775–785. IEEE Computer Society, 2018. doi:10.1109/ICDCS.2018.00080.

[52] Rory Hector, Ramachandran Vaidyanathan, Gokarna Sharma, and Jerry L Trahan. Optimal convex hull formation on a grid by asynchronous robots with lights. *IEEE Transactions on Parallel and Distributed Systems*, 33(12):3532–3545, 2022.

[53] Nojeong Heo and Pramod K Varshney. Energy-efficient deployment of intelligent mobile sensor networks. *IEEE Transactions on Systems, Man, and Cybernetics-Part A: Systems and Humans*, 35(1):78–92, 2004.

[54] Andrew Howard, Maja J Matarić, and Gaurav S Sukhatme. An incremental self-deployment algorithm for mobile sensor networks. *Autonomous Robots*, 13:113–126, 2002.

[55] David Ilcinkas, Ralf Klasing, and Ahmed Mouhamadou Wade. Exploration of constantly connected dynamic graphs based on cactuses. In *21st International Colloquium on Structural Information and Communication Complexity, SIROCCO 2014, Takayama, Japan, July 23-25, 2014. Proceedings*, volume 8576 of *Lecture Notes in Computer Science*, pages 250–262. Springer, 2014. doi:10.1007/978-3-319-09620-9_20.

[56] David Ilcinkas and Ahmed Mouhamadou Wade. On the power of waiting when exploring public transportation systems. In *15th International Conference on Principles of Distributed Systems, OPODIS 2011, Toulouse, France, December 13-16, 2011. Proceedings*, volume 7109 of *Lecture Notes in Computer Science*, pages 451–464. Springer, 2011. doi:10.1007/978-3-642-25873-2_31.

[57] David Ilcinkas and Ahmed Mouhamadou Wade. Exploration of the T-interval-connected dynamic graphs: The case of the ring. In *20th International Colloquium on Structural Information and Communication Complexity, SIROCCO 2013, Ischia, Italy, July 1-3, 2013*, volume 8179 of *Lecture Notes in Computer Science*, pages 13–23. Springer, 2013. doi:10.1007/978-3-319-03578-9_2.

[58] Wayne A Jansen. Intrusion detection with mobile agents. *Computer Communications*, 25(15):1392–1401, 2002.

[59] Aman Kansal, William Kaiser, Gregory Pottie, Mani Srivastava, and Gaurav Sukhatme. Reconfiguration methods for mobile sensor networks. *ACM Transactions on Sensor Networks (TOSN)*, 3(4):22–es, 2007.

[60] George Kantor, Sanjiv Singh, Ronald Peterson, Daniela Rus, Aveek Das, Vijay Kumar, Guilherme Pereira, and John Spletzer. Distributed search and rescue with robot and sensor teams. In *Field and service robotics: Recent advances in reserch and applications*, pages 529–538. Springer, 2006.

[61] Ajay D. Kshemkalyani and Faizan Ali. Efficient dispersion of mobile robots on graphs. In *Proceedings of the 20th International Conference on Dis-*

tributed Computing and Networking, ICDCN 2019, Bangalore, India, January 04-07, 2019, pages 218–227, 2019. doi:10.1145/3288599.3288610.

[62] Ajay D. Kshemkalyani, Anisur Rahaman Molla, and Gokarna Sharma. Fast dispersion of mobile robots on arbitrary graphs. In *Algorithms for Sensor Systems - 15th International Symposium on Algorithms and Experiments for Wireless Sensor Networks, ALGOSENSORS 2019, Munich, Germany, September 12-13, 2019, Revised Selected Papers*, pages 23–40, 2019. doi:10.1007/978-3-030-34405-4_2.

[63] Ajay D. Kshemkalyani, Anisur Rahaman Molla, and Gokarna Sharma. Dispersion of mobile robots in the global communication model. In Nandini Mukherjee and Sriram V. Pemmaraju, editors, *ICDCN 2020: 21st International Conference on Distributed Computing and Networking, Kolkata, India, January 4-7, 2020*, pages 12:1–12:10. ACM, 2020. doi:10.1145/3369740.3369775.

[64] Ajay D. Kshemkalyani, Anisur Rahaman Molla, and Gokarna Sharma. Dispersion of mobile robots on grids. In *WALCOM: Algorithms and Computation - 14th International Conference, WALCOM 2020, Singapore, March 31 - April 2, 2020, Proceedings*, pages 183–197, 2020. doi:10.1007/978-3-030-39881-1_16.

[65] Ajay D. Kshemkalyani, Anisur Rahaman Molla, and Gokarna Sharma. Efficient dispersion of mobile robots on dynamic graphs. In *40th IEEE International Conference on Distributed Computing Systems, ICDCS 2020, Singapore, November 29 - December 1, 2020*, pages 732–742. IEEE, 2020. doi:10.1109/ICDCS47774.2020.00100.

[66] Ajay D. Kshemkalyani and Gokarna Sharma. Near-optimal dispersion on arbitrary anonymous graphs. *CoRR*, abs/2106.03943, 2021. arXiv:2106.03943.

[67] Fabian Kuhn and Rotem Oshman. Dynamic networks: models and algorithms. *SIGACT News*, 42(1):82–96, 2011. doi:10.1145/1959045.1959064.

[68] Xiang Li, M Fikret Ercan, and Yu Fai Fung. Decentralized control for swarm flocking in 3d space. In *Intelligent Robotics and Applications: Second International Conference, ICIRA 2009, Singapore, December 16-18, 2009. Proceedings 2*, pages 744–754. Springer, 2009.

[69] Jie Lin, A Stephen Morse, and Brian DO Anderson. The multi-agent rendezvous problem. In *42nd ieee international conference on decision and control (ieee cat. no. 03ch37475)*, volume 2, pages 1508–1513. IEEE, 2003.

[70] Lit-Hsin Loo, Erwei Lin, Moshe Kam, and Pramod Varshney. Cooperative multi-agent constellation formation under sensing and communication constraints. *Cooperative Control and Optimization*, pages 143–169, 2002.

[71] Giuseppe Antonio Di Luna, Stefan Dobrev, Paola Flocchini, and Nicola Santoro. Distributed exploration of dynamic rings. *Distributed Comput.*, 33(1):41–67, 2020. doi:10.1007/s00446-018-0339-1.

[72] Giuseppe Antonio Di Luna, Paola Flocchini, Sruti Gan Chaudhuri, Federico Poloni, Nicola Santoro, and Giovanni Viglietta. Mutual visibility by luminous robots without collisions. *Inf. Comput.*, 254:392–418, 2017. doi:10.1016/j.ic.2016.09.005.

[73] Giuseppe Antonio Di Luna, Paola Flocchini, Linda Pagli, Giuseppe Prencipe, Nicola Santoro, and Giovanni Viglietta. Gathering in dynamic rings. *Theor. Comput. Sci.*, 811:79–98, 2020. doi:10.1016/j.tcs.2018.10.018.

[74] Subhrangsu Mandal, Anisur Rahaman Molla, and William K. Moses Jr. Live exploration with mobile robots in a dynamic ring, revisited. In *16th International Symposium on Algorithms and Experiments for Wireless Sensor*

Networks, ALGOSENSORS 2020, Pisa, Italy, September 9-10, 2020, volume 12503 of *Lecture Notes in Computer Science*, pages 92–107. Springer, 2020. doi:10.1007/978-3-030-62401-9_7.

[75] Lino Marques, Urbano Nunes, and Anibal T de Almeida. Particle swarm-based olfactory guided search. *Autonomous Robots*, 20:277–287, 2006.

[76] Randolf Menzel and Martin Giurfa. Cognitive architecture of a mini-brain: the honeybee. *Trends in cognitive sciences*, 5(2):62–71, 2001.

[77] Othon Michail and Paul G. Spirakis. Traveling salesman problems in temporal graphs. *Theor. Comput. Sci.*, 634:1–23, 2016. doi:10.1016/j.tcs.2016.04.006.

[78] Anisur Rahaman Molla, Kaushik Mondal, and William K. Moses Jr. Efficient dispersion on an anonymous ring in the presence of weak byzantine robots. In Cristina Maria Pinotti, Alfredo Navarra, and Amitabha Bagchi, editors, *Algorithms for Sensor Systems - 16th International Symposium on Algorithms and Experiments for Wireless Sensor Networks, ALGOSENSORS 2020, Pisa, Italy, September 9-10, 2020, Revised Selected Papers*, volume 12503 of *Lecture Notes in Computer Science*, pages 154–169. Springer, 2020. doi:10.1007/978-3-030-62401-9_11.

[79] Anisur Rahaman Molla, Kaushik Mondal, and William K. Moses Jr. Byzantine dispersion on graphs. In *35th IEEE International Parallel and Distributed Processing Symposium, IPDPS 2021, Portland, OR, USA, May 17-21, 2021*, pages 942–951. IEEE, 2021. doi:10.1109/IPDPS49936.2021.00103.

[80] Anisur Rahaman Molla and William K. Moses Jr. Dispersion of mobile robots: The power of randomness. In *Theory and Applications of Models of Computation - 15th Annual Conference, TAMC 2019, Kitakyushu, Japan, April 13-16, 2019, Proceedings*, pages 481–500, 2019. doi:10.1007/978-3-030-14812-6_30.

[81] Fukuhito Ooshita and Ajoy K. Datta. Brief announcement: Feasibility of weak gathering in connected-over-time dynamic rings. In *20th International Symposium on Stabilization, Safety, and Security of Distributed Systems, SSS 2018, Tokyo, Japan, November 4-7, 2018, Proceedings*, volume 11201 of *Lecture Notes in Computer Science*, pages 393–397. Springer, 2018. doi: 10.1007/978-3-030-03232-6_27.

[82] Linda Pagli, Giuseppe Prencipe, and Giovanni Viglietta. Getting close without touching: near-gathering for autonomous mobile robots. *Distributed Computing*, 28(5):333–349, 2015. doi: 10.1007/s00446-015-0248-5.

[83] Petrisor Panaite and Andrzej Pelc. Exploring unknown undirected graphs. *J. Algorithms*, 33(2):281–295, 1999. doi:10.1006/jagm.1999.1043.

[84] Debasish Pattanayak, Gokarna Sharma, and Partha Sarathi Mandal. Dispersion of mobile robots tolerating faults. In *ICDCN '21: International Conference on Distributed Computing and Networking, Virtual Event, Nara, Japan, January 5-8, 2021, Adjunct Volume*, pages 133–138. ACM, 2021. doi:10.1145/3427477.3429464.

[85] Pavan Poudel, Aisha Aljohani, and Gokarna Sharma. Fault-tolerant complete visibility for asynchronous robots with lights under one-axis agreement. *Theoretical Computer Science*, 850:116–134, 2021.

[86] Pavan Poudel and Gokarna Sharma. Universally optimal gathering under limited visibility. In *International Symposium on Stabilization, Safety, and Security of Distributed Systems*, pages 323–340. Springer, 2017. doi: 10.1007/978-3-319-69084-1_23.

[87] Pavan Poudel and Gokarna Sharma. Time-optimal gathering under limited visibility with one-axis agreement. *Inf.*, 12(11):448, 2021. doi:10.3390/info12110448.

[88] Giuseppe Prencipe and Nicola Santoro. Distributed algorithms for autonomous mobile robots. In *Fourth IFIP International Conference on Theoretical Computer Science-TCS 2006: IFIP 19th Worm Computer Congress,*

TC-1, Foundations of Computer Science, August 23–24, 2006, Santiago, Chile, pages 47–62. Springer, 2006.

[89] Nicola Santoro. Time to change: On distributed computing in dynamic networks (Keynote). In *19th International Conference on Principles of Distributed Systems, OPODIS 2015, December 14-17, 2015, Rennes, France*, volume 46 of *LIPIcs*, pages 3:1–3:14. Schloss Dagstuhl - Leibniz-Zentrum für Informatik, 2015. doi:10.4230/LIPIcs.OPODIS.2015.3.

[90] Gokarna Sharma, Rusul Alsaedi, Costas Busch, and Supratik Mukhopadhyay. The complete visibility problem for fat robots with lights. In *Proceedings of the 19th International Conference on Distributed Computing and Networking*, page 21. ACM, 2018.

[91] Gokarna Sharma, Costas Busch, and Supratik Mukhopadhyay. Bounds on mutual visibility algorithms. In *CCCG*, pages 268–274, 2015.

[92] Gokarna Sharma, Ramachandran Vaidyanathan, Jerry L. Trahan, Costas Busch, and Suresh Rai. Complete visibility for robots with lights in O(1) time. In Borzoo Bonakdarpour and Franck Petit, editors, *Stabilization, Safety, and Security of Distributed Systems - 18th International Symposium, SSS 2016, Lyon, France, November 7-10, 2016, Proceedings*, volume 10083 of *Lecture Notes in Computer Science*, pages 327–345, 2016. doi:10.1007/978-3-319-49259-9_26.

[93] Gokarna Sharma, Ramachandran Vaidyanathan, Jerry L. Trahan, Costas Busch, and Suresh Rai. O(log N)-time complete visibility for asynchronous robots with lights. In *2017 IEEE International Parallel and Distributed Processing Symposium, IPDPS 2017, Orlando, FL, USA, May 29 - June 2, 2017*, pages 513–522. IEEE Computer Society, 2017. doi:10.1109/IPDPS.2017.51.

[94] Takahiro Shintaku, Yuichi Sudo, Hirotsugu Kakugawa, and Toshimitsu Masuzawa. Efficient dispersion of mobile agents without global knowledge. In Stéphane Devismes and Neeraj Mittal, editors, *Stabilization, Safety,*

and Security of Distributed Systems - 22nd International Symposium, SSS 2020, Austin, TX, USA, November 18-21, 2020, Proceedings, volume 12514 of *Lecture Notes in Computer Science*, pages 280–294. Springer, 2020. doi:10.1007/978-3-030-64348-5_22.

[95] Arijit Sil and Sruti Gan Chaudhuri. Line formation by fat robots under limited visibility. *arXiv preprint arXiv:1710.09398*, 2017.

[96] Alexander Spröwitz, Rico Moeckel, Massimo Vespignani, Stéphane Bonardi, and Auke Jan Ijspeert. Roombots: A hardware perspective on 3d self-reconfiguration and locomotion with a homogeneous modular robot. *Robotics and Autonomous Systems*, 62(7):1016–1033, 2014.

[97] Daniel P Stormont. Autonomous rescue robot swarms for first responders. In *CIHSPS 2005. Proceedings of the 2005 IEEE International Conference on Computational Intelligence for Homeland Security and Personal Safety, 2005.*, pages 151–157. IEEE, 2005. doi:10.1109/CIHSPS.2005.1500631.

[98] Kazuo Sugihara and Ichiro Suzuki. Distributed motion coordination of multiple mobile robots. In *Proceedings. 5th IEEE International Symposium on Intelligent Control 1990*, pages 138–143. IEEE, 1990.

[99] Ichiro Suzuki and Masafumi Yamashita. Distributed anonymous mobile robots: Formation of geometric patterns. *SIAM J. Comput.*, 28(4):1347–1363, 1999. doi:10.1137/S009753979628292X.

[100] O Tanaka. Forming a circle by distributed anonymous mobile robots. *Bachelor thesis, Department of Electrical Engineering, Hiroshima University, Hiroshima, Japan*, 1992.

[101] Kasper Thorup, Thomas Alerstam, Mikael Hake, and Nils Kjellén. Bird orientation: compensation for wind drift in migrating raptors is age dependent. *Proceedings of the Royal Society of London. Series B: Biological Sciences*, 270(suppl_1):S8–S11, 2003.

[102] Richard Vaughan, Neil Sumpter, Jane Henderson, Andy Frost, and Stephen Cameron. Experiments in automatic flock control. *Robotics and autonomous systems*, 31(1-2):109–117, 2000.

[103] Hans G Wallraff. *Avian navigation: pigeon homing as a paradigm*. Springer Science & Business Media, 2005.

[104] Guiling Wang, Guohong Cao, and Thomas F La Porta. Movement-assisted sensor deployment. *IEEE Transactions on Mobile Computing*, 5(6):640–652, 2006.

[105] Yukiko Yamauchi and Masafumi Yamashita. Randomized pattern formation algorithm for asynchronous oblivious mobile robots. In *International Symposium on Distributed Computing*, pages 137–151. Springer, 2014.

[106] Xiaoping Yun, Gokhan Alptekin, and Okay Albayrak. Line and circle formation of distributed physical mobile robots. *Journal of Robotic Systems*, 14(2):63–76, 1997.

[107] Zhongyang Zheng and Ying Tan. Group explosion strategy for searching multiple targets using swarm robotic. In *2013 IEEE Congress on Evolutionary Computation*, pages 821–828. IEEE, 2013.